Cambridge Elements

Elements in the Philosophy of Mind
edited by
Keith Frankish
The University of Sheffield

IRRATIONALITY

Ema Sullivan-Bissett
University of Birmingham

CAMBRIDGE
UNIVERSITY PRESS

CAMBRIDGE
UNIVERSITY PRESS

Shaftesbury Road, Cambridge CB2 8EA, United Kingdom

One Liberty Plaza, 20th Floor, New York, NY 10006, USA

477 Williamstown Road, Port Melbourne, VIC 3207, Australia

314–321, 3rd Floor, Plot 3, Splendor Forum, Jasola District Centre,
New Delhi – 110025, India

103 Penang Road, #05–06/07, Visioncrest Commercial, Singapore 238467

Cambridge University Press is part of Cambridge University Press & Assessment,
a department of the University of Cambridge.

We share the University's mission to contribute to society through the pursuit of
education, learning and research at the highest international levels of excellence.

www.cambridge.org
Information on this title: www.cambridge.org/9781009641906

DOI: 10.1017/9781009641883

When citing this work, please include a reference to the DOI 10.1017/9781009641883

First published 2025

A catalogue record for this publication is available from the British Library

ISBN 978-1-009-64190-6 Hardback
ISBN 978-1-009-64192-0 Paperback
ISSN 2633-9080 (online)
ISSN 2633-9072 (print)

Irrationality

Elements in the Philosophy of Mind

DOI: 10.1017/9781009641883
First published online: January 2025

Ema Sullivan-Bissett
University of Birmingham

Author for correspondence: Ema Sullivan-Bissett,
e.l.sullivan-bissett@bham.ac.uk

Abstract: This Element surveys contemporary philosophical and psychological work on various forms of irrationality: akrasia, strange beliefs, and implicit bias. It takes up several questions in an effort to better illuminate these more maligned aspects of human behaviour and cognition: what is rationality? Why is it irrational to act against one's better judgement? Could it ever be rational to do so? What's going wrong with beliefs in conspiracy theories, those arising from self-deception, or those which are classed as delusional? Might some of them in fact be appropriate responses to evidence? Are implicit biases irrational when they conflict with our avowed beliefs? Or might they be rational insofar as they track social realities?

This Element also has a video abstract: Cambridge.org/EPMI_Sullivan

Keywords: irrationality, akrasia, strange belief, implicit bias, evidence

ISBNs: 9781009641906 (HB), 9781009641920 (PB), 9781009641883 (OC)
ISSNs: 2633-9080 (online), 2633-9072 (print)

Contents

1 Introduction

It is commonly thought that rationality is a uniquely human trait. Indeed, that one way of distinguishing humans from non-human animals is via our capacity for rational agency. This idea may well be taken to be 'part of the popular fabric of thought about ourselves' (Rysiew 2008: 1153).

On the other hand, an abundance of psychological studies might challenge the idea that we can be proud of our credentials as (uniquely) rational beings, given that, on the face of it, they seem to reveal that our capacities for rationality leave much to be desired. Empirical support for rational failings abounds. In the Wason selection task, participants are given a rule of the form 'If *a* then *b*', and four double-sided cards, from which they are to decide which *must* be turned over to determine whether the rule is true or false (see Wason 1964 for a version of the task using everyday sentences, and Wason 1966 for an abstract version using letters and numbers). More than 90 per cent of participants fail to identify the correct combination of cards, with the most common errors being the neglect of modus tollens (i.e. neglecting the valid inference if *a* then *b*, not-*b*, so not-*a*), and affirming the consequent (i.e. making the invalid inference if *a* then *b*, *b*, so *a*) (Griggs and Cox 1982: 407).

Another set of experimental results reveal our vulnerability to the conjunction fallacy. The Linda task, first used by Amos Tversky and Daniel Kahneman (1983), is thought to demonstrate poor probabilistic judgement, where most participants (85 per cent) judged that a conjunction (Linda is a bank teller *and* Linda is a feminist) is more probable than just one of its conjuncts (Linda is a bank teller) (297). But here's a logical truth: a conjunction can never be more probable than one of its conjuncts, since a conjunction requires more things to be true of the world (at least two!), whilst a single conjunct is much less demanding, requiring just one thing to be true of the world. Further examples of empirically demonstrated shortcomings include a tendency towards overconfidence (where subjects' confidence in their answers to questions of fact is higher than their accuracy rate), base rate neglect (where subjects making judgements about probabilities underestimate the importance of prior probabilities), and anchoring (where subjects' quantitative guesses are influenced by values at the start of some sequence)[1] (for an overview of the vast literature on

[1] Anchoring is trickier to give a sense of quickly. Tversky and Kahneman (1974) demonstrated this tendency when they asked experimental participants to estimate the sum of a numerical expression. Whilst one group was given the sum $8 \times 7 \times 6 \times 5 \times 4 \times 3 \times 2 \times 1$, another group was given the sum $1 \times 2 \times 3 \times 4 \times 5 \times 6 \times 7 \times 8$. The correct answer to both sums is 40,320. In the first group the median estimate was 2,250, whilst in the second group it was 512 (Tversky and Kahneman 1974: 1128). Although all participants underestimated, the group with the ascending numbers did so to a greater degree – they had their response *anchored* by the lower starting value.

this, see Samuels, Stich, and Faucher 2004, section 2, and Over and Evans 2024, esp. sections 2 and 4).

I won't say too much more about experimental data of this kind in what follows. It turns out that most of us have a less-than-perfect command of the logic of conditionals in certain experimental contexts, and most of us tend to neglect the fact that a conjunction cannot be more probable than its conjuncts. Most of us also fall prey to a whole load of other ways of reasoning which might be thought to depart from ideal rationality. These are interesting enough psychological results, although it is worth noting that these errors don't always generalise. Some work shows that when participants are given equivalent tasks but based on things they care about, they are more likely to arrive at the correct answer. For example, Richard Griggs and James Cox found that when the Wason selection task concerned the legal age for alcohol consumption, 75 per cent of participants (college students) selected the correct answer (compared with 25 per cent for the original task) (Griggs and Cox 1982: 418; see also Wason and Shapiro 1971, Johnson-Laird et al. 1972; compare Manktelow and Evans 1979, Yachanin 1980).

In any case, what a different world we would inhabit were these empirical results the extent of our charge sheet of irrationality! Alas, we have more irrational fish to fry. Let us move from psychological studies demonstrating failures of rationality on certain reasoning tasks, to, perhaps the more interesting and surprising aspects of our mental lives which are often pointed to as paradigmatic cases of irrationality. But first, note that the titles in the Cambridge Elements series are short. Our charge sheet of irrationalities is not. I have thus had to be highly selective in choosing what to include and casualties of my selection are many (e.g. confabulation, distorted memory, positive illusions). I focus on phenomena exemplified by the following examples:

Fred: Against his better judgement, Fred leaves his umbrella at home (he knows it's likely to rain, and that arriving to his meeting wet would be detrimental to landing a business deal).

Jack: Jack believes that *NASA and governments worldwide are covering up the fact that the Earth is flat.*

Katie: Katie believes that *her wife is faithful*, despite strong evidence that she is having an affair.

Glen: Glen believes that *his daughter has been replaced by an imposter.*

Sue: Sue is committed to racial justice and yet interprets neutral behaviour in Malcolm (a Black man) as aggressive. (Were that behaviour performed by a White man she would not ascribe aggression.)

Many of these examples are perfectly commonplace and recognisable. A natural thought about what unites them is that they are all instances of *irrationality*. A more precise thought – and one I hope to make good on as we proceed – is that they are all *taken to be* instances of irrationality, but it is difficult to determine whether that judgement is correct, or, even if it is, what makes it so. I will not give a full account of what it is to be irrational, but let us turn to a brief discussion of what is meant by *irrationality* to set us up for a proper examination of our cases of interest.

2 What Is Irrationality?

2.1 The Domain of Rationality

What kind of thing are we interested in when we're making judgements about what is rational and irrational? We care about the mental and practical lives of human subjects, but not the whole of our mental lives, and not the whole of our practical lives. No one is squabbling over the rationality constraints of day-dreaming about a holiday to Sicily, or how many cloves of garlic one might add to the pasta, or whether one wears blue or red socks on Wednesdays. So which states of mind or behaviours *do* we care about when we're thinking about (ir)rationality?

The easiest category is those states identified as having a *mind-to-world* direction of fit, which is to say, states whose purpose is to *match* the world. Beliefs are the paradigm case. Things go right with my belief that *the pub serves an excellent Riesling*, when it is true that the pub serves an excellent Riesling. Beliefs are prime candidates for rationality assessments, with a standard approach being that when beliefs fail to match the world to an appropriate degree in the appropriate circumstances, we have candidate cases of irrationality. Of course, 'to an appropriate degree in the appropriate circumstances' is where the action is, lest we rule out the bare possibility of rational false belief or irrational true belief. We'll say more about the rationality constraints on belief later (Sections 2.2 and 4).

Alternatively, we might think of those states which have a *world-to-mind* direction of fit, that is, those states whose purpose is to bring it about that the world falls into line with them. The paradigm case of this kind of attitude is *desire*. Things go right with my desire to *have an excellent Riesling this evening* when I do in fact have an excellent Riesling this evening. Whether desires can be rational or irrational is a contentious issue. It is easy enough to make a case for desires being *instrumentally irrational*, that is, being irrational insofar as they prevent one from achieving other goals. For example, I have a desire to go swimming tomorrow morning, but if I succumb to it, I'll miss the deadline for submitting a reference for a student. Is my desire *irrational*? Well, perhaps, insofar as missing the deadline for submitting a reference would be pretty bad for me (if I care about my professional reputation for being reliable, organised, and trustworthy), and even worse for my student (who, presumably, would rather like that job). We might think that the role played by my desire to swim in this unhappy set of circumstances renders that desire *instrumentally irrational.*

But could my desire to go swimming tomorrow morning, or even my desire to do something less noble (stay in bed until midday?), be irrational *by itself*, irrespective of any unfortunate consequences of that desire? The case for *non-instrumentally* irrational desires is tricky, and indeed, some philosophers have denied that there are any such cases (most famously Hume 1739, esp. Part 3, Sect. III; see also Hubin 1990).[2] Although we'll see a role for desire in many of the cases we discuss later, I won't say anything further about whether desires can be non-instrumentally irrational. We'll instead focus on less controversial cases.

Let us turn now to the relationship between rationality and irrationality. A tempting thought is that deviation from what is rational is *irrational*, but we should note that *rational* and *irrational* are (often) *contraries* not *contradictories* (which is to say, they can't *simultaneously characterise* a mental state or action, but the possibility of arationality demonstrates that they can *simultaneously not* characterise a mental state or action). In standard conditions, we might resist the characterisation of my benignly imagining that *I am the World Rubik's Cube Champion* as *rational*, but we'd probably also resist the idea that it's *irrational.* My singing my favourite Elton John song whilst driving to work doesn't look like a *rational* action, but it doesn't look *irrational* either. These cases might be good candidates for arationality, perhaps because there's not an imaginative activity or car-based action in which I ought to have engaged instead. The status of rationality and irrationality as mere contraries looks secure. But when it comes to other areas of my mental life, for example, my patterns of inference, there might be no arational way to proceed. If I believe that *if p then q*, and I also believe that *p*, the inference I draw from these beliefs can only be rational or irrational. I'm rational if I infer that *q*, and I'm irrational if I infer something else (or perhaps, even, if I infer nothing at all) (with the irrationality being more severe if I am occurrently aware of *if p then q* and *p*). In such contexts rationality and irrationality are contradictories.

As will become clear, many of the cases we'll look at more closely resemble what we want to say about inference than what we want to say about my

[2] Shannon Spaulding (2015) explores whether we might model the non-instrumental rationality of desire by appeal to rationality constraints on belief, a possibility in which she finds little mileage (470–5).

imaginative tendencies towards my Rubik's cube credentials, or my singing along to Elton John. That is, our cases are ones where a more rational belief or action suggests itself. They are cases where a natural thought is that, speaking from a standpoint of rationality, our subjects could have done better. Given this, we'll proceed by identifying what makes a person, mental state, or action *rational* and see the failure to meet such conditions as our route into irrationality.

2.2 The Standard Picture

Let us begin with what has been called the *Standard Picture of rationality*, which we will refer back to throughout the Element.

> [T]o be rational is to reason in accordance with principles of reasoning that are based on rules of logic, probability theory, and so forth. (Stein 1997: 4)

Adopting this Standard Picture naturally gives rise to what has been called the 'pessimistic interpretation' of the experimental results mentioned in the Introduction (Samuels, Stich, and Faucher 2004: 132). When experimental participants fail the Wason selection task, they fail to correctly apply the logic of conditionals. When experimental participants take it to be more likely that Linda is not only a bank teller but also one of the feminist variety, they misunderstand how probability works. With the Standard Picture in hand, we are left with 'bleak implications' when we turn to 'the rationality of the man and woman in the street' (Samuels, Stich, and Faucher 2004: 132). Of course, the Standard Picture also explains why we conclude that the experimental participants were selecting their cards or making their probability judgements in an *irrational way*; they were doing so against principles of reasoning we take to be constitutive of rationality.

Sometimes the relevant principles can't be so straightforwardly understood as ones embodying proper appreciation of the formal rules of logic and probability theory.[3] How we understand the principles operative in such cases will depend on what kind of rationality we're interested in, and what kind of thing it characterises (or not). It is common to distinguish two broad kinds of rationality: *practical* rationality and *epistemic* (or *theoretical*) rationality. Very roughly, practical rationality is concerned with our actions, whilst epistemic rationality

[3] José Bermúdez (2001) objects to the Standard Picture on the grounds that it focuses on procedural rationality (i.e. formal rules of logic) with neglect of 'the role in evaluating rationality of norms of good reasoning' (464). Thus, I may well be exhibiting a bit of philosophical license in reading the Standard Picture's talk of 'principles of reasoning' broadly. That is, I have taken them to include rationality constraints on belief and action that go beyond what formal rules of logic would recommend. We can simply stipulate this broader reading given that our project is one of moving from ideas of irrationality to illuminating apparent instances of it.

takes as its remit our mental lives, and looks to the rationality of various cognitions – most obviously beliefs.

Let us turn to the kinds of cases that we'll be focusing on – does the Standard Picture help us get a grip on what's going wrong in such cases? Fred acts against his better judgement in leaving his umbrella at home. It is standard to think of cases like Fred's as cases of *practical* irrationality. What 'principles of reasoning' does he fail to act in accordance with? A natural thought is that the practical reasoning underlying our action should issue in judgements concerning *what to do* which match our judgements about *what it is best or better to do*. Cases like Fred's, where these things come apart, are said to be ones of *weakness of will* or *akrasia*.

Return to our cases of strange belief (Jack's belief that there is a global cover-up of the fact that *the Earth is flat*, Katie's belief that *her wife is faithful*, Glen's belief that *his daughter has been replaced by an imposter*). Here the irrationality involved is of the *epistemic* variety. What principles are our protagonists failing to follow in forming their beliefs? Several rationality constraints on belief have been suggested, including consistency (one should not hold inconsistent beliefs) and inferential coherence (one should believe that which follows from beliefs already held). We'll look at our cases in the light of these principles later. Perhaps the most obvious constraint on belief's rationality concerns its having the appropriate relationship to evidence. Belief that is rational is belief formed *in response to* sufficient evidence, and which is *sensitive to* counterevidence. Jack, Katie, and Glen, we can suppose, all have beliefs which fail on both sides of the coin. Jack's belief is based on poor evidence: testimony from scientifically illiterate friends and untrustworthy news sources, and is insensitive to the overwhelming evidence that the Earth is in fact a sun-orbiting sphere. Katie's belief is based on her attending to the very thin evidence base for fidelity, perhaps her wife's continued (albeit infrequent) expressions of love, whilst being insensitive to her coming home late, taking middle-of-the-night phone calls, a loss of interest in their intimate life, and so on. Glen's belief is based on the very strange experience he has when looking at his daughter but is insensitive to the large body of evidence against his claim – the supposed imposter knows things only his daughter could know, no one else suspects her, and so on. Our cases of strange belief have in common, at the very least, an improper relationship to evidence.

What are we to say of Sue, some of whose actions look to be contrary to her firmly held and avowed egalitarian beliefs? In cases of *implicit bias*, the locus of irrationality is difficult to identify without first attending to what implicit bias *is*, and so I reserve that work for later (Section 5).

I've gestured at the kinds of things which might ground judgements of irrationality for our range of cases, of which we'll say much more as we proceed. Before that, I'll briefly address two distinctions regarding rationality, as well as two debates arising from the proper understanding and application of it.

2.3 Structural versus Substantive Rationality

Earlier I distinguished between *epistemic* and *practical* rationality. A different way of carving up the space of possibilities is suggested by the distinction between *structural* and *substantive rationality*. Benjamin Kiesewetter and Alex Worsnop understand *structural rationality* to concern combinations of attitudes (or the absence of combinations). This means that we can make assessments of structural rationality without knowing anything of the subject's situation, and indeed, without even knowing the contents of her attitude(s). For example, we know that a subject who believes that *p* and believes that not-*p* is irrational. We can make that judgement without having to know about her circumstances, without having to know what *p* denotes, and indeed without having to know which of the two attitudes she ought to reject (Kiesewetter and Worsnip 2023, section 1.2). *Substantive rationality* on the other hand, has none of these features, and is thought instead to relate to normative reasons, including those suggested by the weight of evidence. For example, we can denote the belief that *grass is green* and the delusional belief that *my son is an imposter* in the same way, namely, as the belief *that p*. Once we do so, though, we can no longer tell whether the belief is rational or not. In substantive cases then, the irrationality arises from what *p* denotes, whilst in structural cases it arises from relations between attitudes, regardless of what *p* denotes.

We'll see that the irrationality attributed to subjects throughout our examples is of both the structural and the substantive kind. Sometimes our judgements of irrationality will be grounded in a subject having inconsistent attitudes, or their behaving in ways which diverge from their best judgement (structural irrationality). Other times they will be grounded in the subject's attitudes having an inappropriate relationship to the evidence (substantive irrationality). As it happens, the project of this Element is not better served by explicitly carving these kinds of rationality up, particularly given that the distinction is not uncontroversial (Kiesewetter and Worsnip 2023, section 1.3). For this reason, the distinction won't play a role in the discussions that follow.

2.4 Ideal versus Bounded Rationality

So far we have sought to get a handle on what makes a mental state or action rational by appeal to the Standard Picture, which has it that rationality consists in reasoning in accordance with certain principles. What we're doing in these cases is holding our target mental state or action up to the light of these principles and seeing whether it measures up. When it comes to assessing the rationality of belief, doing so in this way might be interpreted as a project of *ideal epistemology*, that is, a project 'concerned with questions about what perfectly rational, cognitively idealized, computationally unlimited believers would believe' (Carr 2022: 1132). It is against this standard that we evaluate the subjects in some of our examples as irrational.

But is this standard a fair one? No one thinks that there is, in fact, a perfectly rational human agent, and so why would an imagined construction of one be the relevant standard against which to evaluate the rationality of our epistemic lives? This thought might make attractive a different approach, that of *non-ideal* or *bounded epistemology*. According to this framework, in assessing the rationality or otherwise of some cognition, we should recognise our cognitive limitations, or *bounds*.[4]

David Thorstad (2024) suggests two ways of understanding the disagreement between ideal and bounded epistemologists concerned with rationality. A weaker way is to understand the two approaches as engaged in different but compatible normative projects, and the bounded epistemologist's only plea is that we should accommodate facts about our bounds in order to get at a *full* picture of human rationality. A stronger reading of the disagreement has it that we have two incompatible descriptive projects, which, in some cases, in seeking to describe something as *rational* (or not), come to different judgements. There is only one type of rationality, and it is *either* ideal *or* bounded (397–8).

The project in the following sections is not one which opts for either approach. We'll be looking at the etiology of particular kinds of cognition, and seeking to evaluate them against their typical contexts of manifestation. There may be some explanatory projects which play better with one approach over the other. For example, Jennifer Carr (2022) has argued that '[i]f we want a normatively robust theory of epistemic rationality, ideal epistemology is the only game in town' (1131).[5] Such a project is not, of course, the focus of this Element.

---

[4] Another departure from an idealised approach can be found in the programme of *ecological rationality*. Proponents point out that other, 'traditional' approaches will proceed by identifying single optimal cognitive strategies, without attending to the environmental contexts in which they might be successful (or not) (Todd and Gigerenzer 2012: 14; Hertwig et al. 2022: 468). Instead, we should look at the *fit* between certain strategies and their operation in particular kinds of environment (Todd and Gigerenzer 2012: 24). Sometimes heuristics which eschew computation and the gathering of information can be better than more complex strategies (Todd and Gigerenzer 2012: 30; see Sullivan-Bissett *forthcoming* for more general discussion of evolutionary pressures on belief capacities).

[5] Robin McKenna (2023) has argued that ideal epistemologists are in fact at risk of 'constructing an inadequate epistemology' insofar as 'they often end up proposing intellectual goals and norms of

As we proceed we will identify departures from ideal rationality. However, in our seeking to illuminate paradigmatic instances of irrationality, we will look at the broader context. Doing so is open to epistemologists of both stripes – the ideal epistemologist may well accept that, for example, a given belief was *understandable* or *all-things-considered forgivable*, but will just maintain that those evaluations ought not to move us from our judgement that it is nevertheless *irrational*. The bounded epistemologist may demur, having it that particular features of the broader context ought to make us reflect on our initial characterisation of our target belief *as irrational*. Sometimes our discussions take a bounded bent, but may be translated without much trouble into language friendlier to an ideal project.

2.5 Pragmatic Encroachment

Earlier (Section 2.2), in trying to capture what might make some beliefs irrational, we noted constraints including consistency, inferential coherence, and a belief's relationship to evidence (and counterevidence). Whatever is said here about the rationality or otherwise of belief, it is coming firmly from epistemic quarters. That is, it is common to take it that non-epistemic considerations are not (and cannot be) reasons for belief, or things to which we might appeal in assessing the rationality of belief.[6]

However, some philosophers have argued for the importance of recognising *pragmatic encroachment* in our epistemic lives. This is the idea that practical considerations should make a difference to our epistemic evaluations. Most commonly, the notion has been applied to knowledge ascription. This tends to be motivated by taking a low-stakes case to which we would happily ascribe knowledge, and then significantly raising the practical costs of being wrong, at which point, say the pragmatic encroachers, we should not ascribe knowledge after all (Kvanvig 2011: 77–8).[7]

---

inquiry that are not only unattainable but such that, in trying to attain or follow them, we are likely to worsen rather than improve our epistemic situation' (20).

[6] Recent challenges to this approach should be noted. Susanna Rinard (2017) argues that we should assess the rationality of belief in the same way as we assess the rationality of other states, and not take it to be determined solely by epistemic considerations (most notably, *evidential* ones) (see also McCormick 2015, Leary 2017).

[7] The most commonly discussed case of this kind is Keith DeRose's bank case (1992: 913). My partner and I had planned to drop into the bank on Friday evening to deposit our pay cheques. Noticing long queues, I suggest returning Saturday morning. My partner notes that banks often close on Saturdays, and asks if I am sure that ours will be open. In one version of the story, there is little hanging on when we deposit our pay cheques. I reply that the bank will be open – citing as evidence a recent Saturday morning visit. In another version of the story, it's crucial that the money hits our account by the end of the weekend, lest there be extremely unfortunate consequences. Now when my partner asks if I'm sure that our bank will be open on Saturday morning, I hesitate, and decide to check to confirm their opening hours. According to DeRose (1992), in the

More saliently for us, it has been argued that there can also be pragmatic encroachment on the justification or rationality of belief. For example, Mark Schroeder argues that we can understand how there can be pragmatic encroachment on knowledge by understanding the practical factors we take to defeat knowledge to do so *by* defeating epistemic rationality (Schroeder 2012: 266).[8] If the pragmatic encroachers are right, then we take too narrow a view of epistemic rationality when we understand it to be grounded purely in epistemic considerations.

We need take no stand on this issue, since in the cases we discuss the considerations which go into our assessments of rationality will be grounded only in the epistemic. There won't be much by way of practical considerations which could plausibly encroach, even for those sympathetic to the idea of such a possibility (see fn. 8 for a notable exception).

2.6 Epistemic Innocence

Finally, let's turn briefly to a recent research programme led by Lisa Bortolotti. It has been commonplace in the literature on epistemically imperfect cognitions to endorse what Bortolotti calls the *trade-off view* of practical benefits and epistemic harms (Bortolotti 2020: 125). That is, practical benefits come at the cost of epistemic ones. Bortolotti challenges this and offers a new way of thinking about epistemically imperfect cognitions, which is to use the framework of *epistemic innocence*. This framework promises to provide a more nuanced look at the relationship between epistemic and practical harms and benefits. To say that, for example, a belief is *epistemically innocent*, is not to say that it is thus *rational*, but only to say that it is due more epistemic credit than traditional frameworks might allow. Sometimes imperfect cognitions can be seen as emergency responses and, though epistemically irrational, can deliver epistemic benefits that would not be available were the subject to have the more epistemically rational cognition. A case for epistemic innocence has been made most robustly and generally in Bortolotti's 2020 book, as well as specifically for delusions (Bortolotti 2015b, 2016; Sullivan-Bissett 2018), confabulatory explanation (Sullivan-Bissett 2015; Bortolotti 2018), psychedelic states (Letheby 2015), inaccurate social cognition (Puddifoot 2017), and clinical memory distortions (Bortolotti and Sullivan-Bissett 2020). I won't

first version I know that the bank will be open on Saturday morning, and in the second version I do not. This is *contextualism* about knowledge attribution, which has it that sentences of the form 'S knows that *p*' have truth conditions that vary depending on the context (914).

[8] Jie Gao has argued that some cases of self-deception are ones where there is pragmatic encroachment on epistemic rationality, in such a way as to make the self-deceptive belief a rational one. Gao has it that her cases of self-deception are best understood as rational against a background of bounded rationality but irrational against a background of ideal rationality (Gao 2020: 29).

discuss this notion any further, because it doesn't go directly to our assessments of rationality. It does, though, serve as a reminder of the often complex and dynamic relationships held between irrational cognition and the contexts in which it occurs.

2.7 Concluding Remarks

We end our quick tour of rationality and irrationality here and move onto what are taken to be some of its paradigmatic instances. We might have taken a different approach which instead considered what various phenomena could tell us about the idea of irrationality, or even about the possibility of a perfectly rational being, or how it is that we might better live up to norms of rationality in our practical and mental lives. Thinking about instances of irrationality present in human psychology could be insightful to these broader, more abstract questions (for an example of this approach, see Bortolotti 2015a). This Element will come at the topic from a different angle. We'll look closely at various kinds of cases and seek to come to an understanding of them by reflecting on their status as irrational. We'll examine what it is about our cases that makes it proper to understand them in this way, and, where appropriate, we'll question whether their reputation for being instances of irrationality is a fair one. In any case, my hope is that the discussions which follow will help the reader towards a better understanding of some of the more maligned aspects of our practical and mental lives.

3 Akrasia

3.1 What Is Akrasia?

As with so many phenomena to which the philosopher might direct her thinking, there is no uncontroversial characterisation of *akrasia* on which we can base the following discussion. The phenomenon of interest is also often called *weakness of will*, although some philosophers have argued that it is important to keep these two notions apart.[9] Before characterising akrasia in a minimally contentious way, let us, for the sake of contrast, say something about the non-akratic case. A natural (if over-simplistic) thought is that our actions are caused by some practical judgement concerning what to do, and that one's practical judgement aligns with one's *better judgement* (i.e. one's judgement about what it is *best or better to do*).[10] What is meant by one's *better judgment*? We

[9] Amelie Rorty describes the identification of akrasia and weakness of will as 'profoundly misleading' on the grounds that the 'akratic break' need not involve weakness of will (Rorty 1980: 333, n.*, see also Holton 1999).

[10] Some authors have captured akratic actions as those actions against one's better judgement, understood as a judgement that a given action is *better* (even if not *the best*) (Davidson 1982: 21–2, Audi 1990: 271). I follow this approach although sometimes it will be easier to talk of *best* actions rather than *better* ones.

can follow Nomy Arpaly (2000) in understanding it as referring to 'the judgment that one reaches, having taken into account all the reasons one judges to be relevant, as to what would be best for one to do in a given situation' (490). Now consider Figure 1 (where '=' picks out that the same action is recommended by one's practical judgement and one's better judgement, and the downward arrow represents one's practical judgement as the cause of one's action).

In this highly simplified and idealised set-up, I form a practical judgement, of the form *I shall do a*, which aligns with my better judgement that *it is better to do a*. My practical judgement is the basis for my action, *a*, which is also the action recommended by my better judgement.

Let us turn now to akrasia, beginning with what Robert Audi identifies as 'a common element' in various accounts, that of *acting against one's better judgement* (1990: 270).[11] In cases of akrasia then, our schematic looks like this (Figure 2) (where '≠' picks out that the action recommended by one's practical judgement is different from that recommended by one's better judgement).

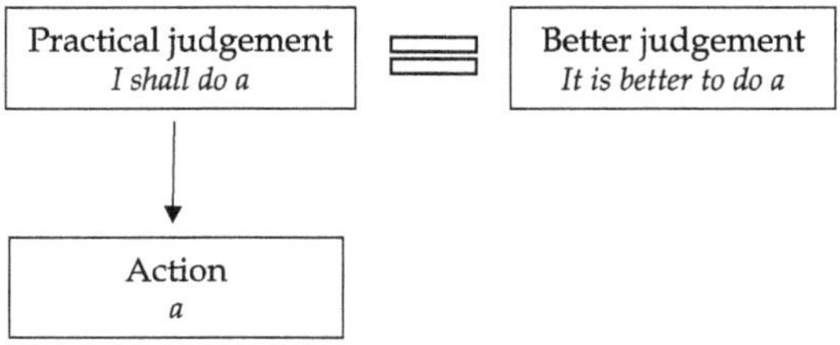

Figure 1 The non-akratic agent.

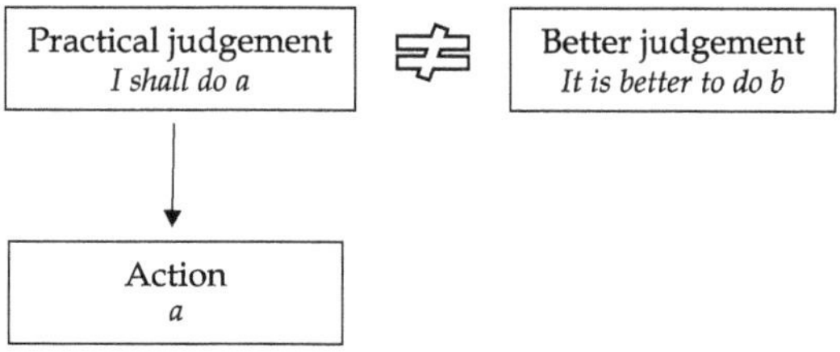

Figure 2 The akratic agent.

[11] Talk in terms of *acting against one's better judgement* is common, but not universal. For example, Richard Holton (2009) has argued that cases of action arising from weakness of will (which he distinguishes from *akrasia*) are better understood as cases in which people *fail to act on their intentions*, more specifically, when those intentions are insufficiently resistant to reconsideration (see also McIntyre 2006, Dodd 2009). Putative cases of weakness of will without acting against one's better judgement motivate this kind of approach, with such cases analysed in terms of *revising an intention one ought not to have revised*.

On this picture, our action is caused by a practical judgement which does not align with our better judgement. What is it to *act against* one's better judgement so understood? Here we can lay out four jointly sufficient conditions for so acting (adapted from Audi 1990: 270).

For a subject *S* to act against her better judgement in performing action *a*, *S*:

1. Performs action *a* intentionally
2. Has judged that an alternative action, *b*, is better than *a*
3. Has not abandoned the judgement that an alternative action, *b*, is better than *a*
4. Is aware that she has judged that *b* would be better than *a*, and that she maintains this judgement.

Return to our earlier case of Fred, who judges that *it would be better to take his umbrella*. He has a big day at work schmoozing clients, involving taking them to lunch, followed by a walk along the canal, and (if all goes well), closing the deal over wine at a lavish bar. He thinks he will look credible and trustworthy in his new suit but takes this overall look to be significantly compromised should he carry his umbrella, and so resigns to take his chances, leaving the umbrella at home. However, a rainstorm is forecast, and the mildly deleterious effect on his overall look of carrying an umbrella would pale in comparison with the hugely deleterious effect of arriving to meet his clients dripping wet, or so negligently opening himself up to the elements partway through their encounter. He knows that carrying an umbrella is an annoyance, particularly if the forecast is wrong. He will need to remember where he puts it down as he goes about his day, and its bright pink colour really doesn't set the suit off in a way one might hope of an accessory. Nevertheless, when considering the information available to him, Fred judges that *it would be better to take his umbrella*. Now imagine that Fred goes off to work without his umbrella. In doing so, Fred has performed an action *against his better judgement* (schematised in Figure 3).

Let us turn to why the four conditions specified earlier are required for us to make good on this characterisation of Fred's action.

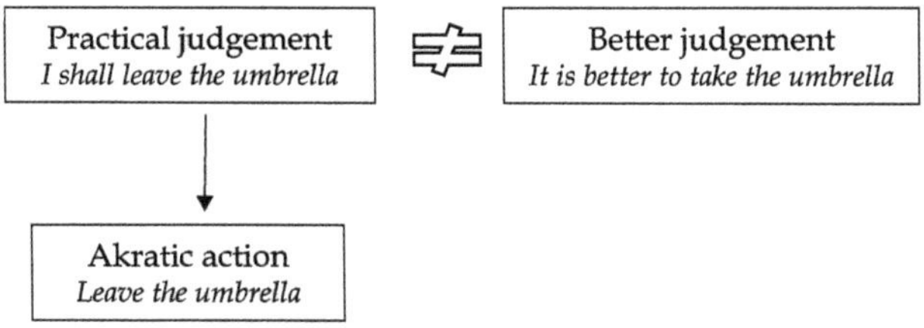

Figure 3 The case of akratic Fred.

Imagine that Fred went off to work without his umbrella *unintentionally*, that is, he simply forgot to grab it on the way out of the door. If the umbrella was left for this reason, we would withdraw our claim that Fred acted *against* his better judgement, although his action was of course *inconsistent with* it. We see then the necessity of condition (1), the action must be performed *intentionally* for it to be akratic.

Now imagine that Fred does not judge that *it would be better to take his umbrella*, and, indeed, does not take it. The case could be otherwise identical – a rainstorm is forecast, Fred knows this, but weighing everything up he fails to judge *that taking his umbrella would be better than not taking it*. Perhaps the colour clash with his outfit weighs on him, or perhaps he engages in motivated reasoning and comes to believe that *it will not rain*. It might well be that we, as neutral observers, take it to be obvious that Fred should take his umbrella, and we judge him harshly for not coming to this judgement. But if he really doesn't come to this judgement, there is no akratic action in his failing to take his umbrella. Condition (2) is also necessary.

Now imagine that Fred *did* judge that *it would be better to take his umbrella*, but has since abandoned that judgement. Perhaps his evidence base has changed (rain is no longer forecast), or perhaps the reasons given previously for not forming the judgement in the first place now strike him, and he revises the judgement. On further consideration, prompted by the sight of himself in the mirror carrying what now seems comically ill-suited to accessorise his outfit, he revises his judgment that *it would be best to take his umbrella* – and with a knowing reckless abandon, invites the chips to fall where they may. Given this revision, Fred's action of leaving the umbrella at home would not be akratic. Condition (3) is required.[12]

Finally, condition (4) has it that Fred must be aware of conditions (2) and (3), that is, he must be aware that he has formed the judgement *that it would be better to take his umbrella* (condition 2), and he must be aware that his judgement has not changed (condition 3). Not being aware of (2) is easy enough – we can imagine that Fred judged that *it would be better to take his*

12 Following Alison McIntyre, we can distinguish *rationalising Fred* (who rationalises leaving his umbrella, deciding that it is best to do so after all) from *akratic Fred* (who leaves the umbrella without having revised his judgement that *it would be better to take it*). For McIntyre (2006), whatever we take to be going wrong with rationalising Fred seems rather close to what is going wrong with akratic Fred (286). Fred himself may not be able to tell whether he continues to judge that *it is best to take his umbrella*, or, having glanced at himself in the mirror, whether he has rationalised his decision not to do so. If what's going wrong with akratic Fred is his failing to constrain the influence of particular motives or desires on his practical judgement, rationalising Fred is guilty of the same sin (287).

umbrella, but then, through sheer forgetfulness or some more sinister memory-inhibiting event, simply forgot that he had judged this. And so, he leaves his umbrella at home. Doing so would not be akratic.

How should we understand what it would take to not be aware of (3), that is, for Fred not to be aware that he continues to judge that *it would be best to take his umbrella*? Fred not being aware that there is this judgement *that he still holds* is tricky, and gets us into territory about the nature of judgement. It is much easier to suppose that one could forget that one *had* judged, than that one could forget that one *continues to judge*. That is because it is commonplace to think that judgement is necessarily occurrent, or at the very least, that the judgement we're interested in when thinking about akrasia is necessarily occurrent. If that's right, then it would make little sense to suppose that Fred both (a) continues to hold the judgement and (b) is not aware that he continues to hold the judgement. This complication aside, we can see, I hope, even if it is hard to specify what it would mean for Fred not to be aware of a judgement he still holds, that Fred would need to be aware of his judgement, and of his maintaining it, to count as acting akratically.

Before turning to the rationality or otherwise of akratic action, I speak briefly to *possibility*. It might seem strange to ask whether akratic action is possible, having apparently (and thoroughly!) specified an example of that very thing. However, some authors have argued that akratic action is impossible, and, put simply, that's because they see a very close relationship between judgements about what it is better for one to do, and decisions made about what is actually done (see, for example, Donald Davidson's (1980) paradox of akrasia (23)). It might be thought that if I *really* judge that *it is better to perform action b*, then *it follows from that judgement*, all else equal, that *I will perform action b*.

Let us make explicit a presumption only implicit so far: akrasia stands up as an interesting phenomenon only to the extent that we take settling the question regarding *what one will do* as answered by settling *what it is best or better for one to do*. Without this, akrasia would be no more interesting than the fact that my judgement about what would be the most *fun* thing to do fails to bring about action in line with that judgement. Being the *best* action would simply take its place alongside other candidate actions recommended by their credentials in a given dimension, for example, that which is the most *fun*, or the most *outrageous*. Rejecting this implicit presumption would be to sever the link between judgements about what it is best to do with the practical reasoning that underlies what is in fact done. Akratic action would thus be possible, and more than that, not especially remarkable. Fred judges that *it would be better to take his umbrella*, but he also judges that *it would be fashionable not to*. Fashion simply won the day. This approach has been rejected by some philosophers on the grounds that severing the link between judgements about what is best with the practical reasoning underlying what is done is 'too high a price to pay' (Bratman 1979: 159).

A more nuanced route to establishing the possibility of akrasia involves modelling the relationship between two judgements: the action-prompting judgement which is the conclusion of practical reasoning, and the judgement about what it is best to do. Specifically, to make space for akratic action, we must be able to separate the two. Michael Bratman does this by casting the conclusions reached in practical reasoning as non-evaluative, and those reached by one's better judgement as evaluative (Bratman 1979: 162). He has it that in failing to transition from the evaluative conclusion to the non-evaluative conclusion, one commits no 'extreme logical error' suggestive of impossibility (Bratman 1979: 164).

Another approach is to distinguish between the judgement that an action is prima facie better, and a judgement that an action is *all things considered* better (Davidson 1980). In a case of akrasia where a subject's better judgement is that x is better, but nevertheless she does y, the judgement that x is better is an *all things considered* judgement (one relative to the subject's background beliefs and values she takes to be relevant to the case). A judgement of this kind is conditional (on the appropriateness of the beliefs and values that inform it). The competing judgement that causes the agent to y instead of x, is an *unconditional* judgement, and judgements of this kind are the ones that prompt action.

Our discussion of possibility has been extremely brief, but our end point represents what Sarah Stroud and Christine Tappolet (2003) have identified as 'two general points of consensus' in the contemporary literature on this topic: (1) that akrasia is possible, and it is so (2) '*only as a species of practical irrationality*' (5). Let us turn then to assessing the (ir)rationality of akratic action.

3.2 Akrasia and (Ir)rationality

On one construal of what is going on in these cases, what is to be explained is why the akratic subject moves from considerations in favour of the akratic action a to the practical judgement 'I shall do a', *given* her recognition of considerations in favour of b, where the latter considerations are such as to recommend b over a as the best (or better) action. This is Bratman's conception of the cognitive architecture, and he takes this transition to be perfectly possible, given his view of the nature of practical reasoning. However, in saving the possibility of akratic action, Bratman doesn't say much about how we might explain this possible but irrational transition.

Similarly, Davidson's theory of practical reasoning makes akratic action possible, but irrational. Davidson suggests that the rational subject will, in her application of practical reasoning, be guided by the *principle of continence* which has it that one should 'perform the action judged best on the basis of all available relevant reasons' (Davidson 1980: 41). We are left not with questions of possibility, but with questions concerning why an agent would act in such and such a way, given the set of judgements involved. Why would anyone act in such a way as to be out of step with the principle of continence?

For Davidson, reason calls for Fred to carry his umbrella, the chances of rain are significant, arriving at the important meeting drowned will be a very bad look indeed and is likely to have undesirable professional consequences. But that pink umbrella really does look a bit silly carried against this rather expensive suit, it's quite annoying having to carry it, weather forecasts are sometimes wrong ... If Fred were not akratic, he would not give way to these latter considerations. But Fred is akratic, and he does. Why so? Davidson (1980) suggests that in seeking a psychological explanation of akratic action, we'll find ourselves referring to otherwise familiar phenomena including 'self-deception, overpowering desires, lack of imagination, and the rest' (42).

The saving of akrasia from the grips of impossibility then does not wrap things up very neatly. We may have answered the question of whether akratic action is possible (yes), and we have done so by theorising about the architecture of practical reasoning, driving a gap between the judgements which motivate action, and those which represent one's better judgement. Although we have found a gap, it is a small one, often bridged by what are taken to be principles of rational practical reasoning. These principles link together that which akratic action pulls apart – judgements that motivate action and judgements about how to act. That small gap has become what is to be explained, and that explanation will look different in each case because a whole range of standard resources are available to explain why we sometimes irrationally fail to have our actions align with what we judge it is better to do. Perhaps Fred convinces himself that today is the day the weather forecast will be wrong, or his desire to not offset his suit with a pink accessory is overpowering when he glimpses himself in the mirror. Our task now is to build explanations for why Fred allows for the gap exploited by akrasia in his practical reasoning.

There's something mildly unsatisfying about this, if one starts from the idea that akratic action is a special form of irrationality demanding a particular explanation. If our explanation of the irrationality involved piggybacks on that involved in other areas of our mental lives, akratic action is not an especially interesting token of the type. The irrationality involved in akrasia might in fact strike us as rather pedestrian.

If one is in the market for something a bit more exciting to say, we might find what we're looking for in some philosophers' opposition to the idea that akrasia is always irrational, an idea which, as Audi (1990) observes, no philosopher '[had] seriously criticised' (270). A decade later we hear a similar complaint from Arpaly (2000) who states that akratic action as *irrational* is largely uncontested: 'it is almost a universal assumption in contemporary philosophy [. . .] that acting against one's best judgement is never an instance of rational action' (490–1). Both Audi and Arpaly argue that at least some akratic actions are properly taken as *rational*, or at least, *more rational* than alternative actions, and they each take this idea to have not been given due attention.

One way of making good on this is to take a wider view of rationality, rather than having it that our better judgements are the ones that inform, or should inform, our action. On such a picture, action out of line with those judgements straightforwardly falls out as irrational. Audi (1990) offers the following counterexample:

> *John*: a practised and conscientious retributivist. He believes that he should punish his daughter for talking hours on the phone when she knew she should study. On reflection, he judges that he should deny her a Saturday outing. But a day later, when it comes time to deny her the outing, he looks into her eyes, realises that she will be quite upset, decides to make do with a stern rebuke, and lets her go. He feels guilty and chides himself. It is not that he changed his mind; he was simply too uncomfortable with the prospect of cracking down. Suppose, however, that he also has a strong standing belief that he must be a reasonable parent and is well aware that the deprivation would hurt the child and cause a rebellious reaction. He might be so disposed that if he had thought long enough about the matter, he would have changed his mind; but that is perfectly consistent with the assumption that if his will were stronger, he would have punished her. (276–7)

Audi has it that John's case is one of akratic – but not irrational – action. Although John's better judgement – informed by his retributive desires – is that *he should punish his daughter*, it would be to take too narrow a look at the situation to characterise his not punishing his daughter as irrational purely for being out of line with that judgement. In John's case, the rational basis for his better judgement is 'outweighed by the larger rational considerations producing the incontinent action' which also render the action rational after all (277).

Audi (1990) advocates pulling away from the model which grounds rationality on the appropriate transition between one's better judgement and the conclusion of practical reasoning. Instead, a more holistic approach should inform our assessment of when an action is rational, taking into account 'sufficiently good reasons of the agent', even when those reasons are not part of the judgement concerning the action that would be best (or better) (278–9). Akrasia's relative rarity is down to the fact that usually our overall reasons are reflected in our judgements about what is best, but sometimes such judgements pull away from our deepest beliefs and desires. If we give way to these deepest beliefs and desires, opting for the action recommended by them rather than our better judgement, we engage in akratic action which is not irrational.

Another way to separate akratic action and irrationality is suggested by Arpaly (2000), whose argument begins by drawing attention to cases of epistemically rational belief formation in the absence of deliberation, which she refers to as cases of *dawning*. It would take us too far afield to lay out detailed examples (as Arpaly does), so let us follow her in understanding these cases as ones in which 'people change their minds, sans deliberation, as a result of a long period of exposure to new evidence' (508). At least some cases of dawning are ones in which 'we regard people as rational despite the fact that their rationality is not the product of deliberation' (509). Arpaly asks:

> why should it be any stranger to claim that [akratic subjects] are moved to action rationally, for good reasons, as a legitimate response to good evidence of which they are aware, even though they do not deliberate their way into their actions? (510)

We are invited to see akratic action as arising in a way akin to cases of belief change via *dawning*, which is non-deliberative, and sometimes rational. If non-deliberative belief change is not always irrational (and even sometimes rational), why not non-deliberative action? That's a fine question, and Arpaly is surely right that we would need a reason to rule out the possibility of something rational arising out of a non-deliberative process in the action case if we allow it in the belief case. The plausibility of this for akratic action will depend on whether we think such cases are properly characterised as ones of *action without deliberation*.[13] Arpaly (2000) thinks they are:

> A rational agent's manual is a deliberator's manual, and acting against one's best judgment is not the sort of thing one settles on doing as a result of *good*

[13] Arpaly (2000) characterises akrasia as failing to do *a*, when one judges that one should do *a* (490). There is no requirement that *one is aware that one has judged that a would be better, and that one maintains this judgement* (condition (4) from our earlier discussion, Section 3.1). Perhaps it is the presence of a condition of this kind which puts us in mind of the deliberative realm, and its absence in Arpaly's characterisation of akrasia that allows her to step outside of it.

> *deliberation*. [. . .] Acting against one's best judgment is not something that one can, as a result of *deliberation*, resolve to do; one just changes one's best judgment as to what to do. (490, my emphasis)

There's a move here from *good deliberation* to *deliberation* (as italicised), but the rational agent's manual presumably doesn't delineate all that is *possible* with us cognitively (lest we run together irrationality with impossibility). Putting that aside though, is it accurate to understand akratic action as not arising from deliberation? Personally, this strikes me as a rather revisionary take.

Our discussion so far is one that may well be interpreted as taking akratic action as the output of a process of deliberation over what to do, indeed, perhaps the interest of akrasia precisely stems from framing it *as arising from deliberation*. How can one's practical judgement concerning *what to do* (which gives rise to action) diverge from one's judgement about *what it would be better to do*? How can one *decide to* do *a* whilst at the same time recognising that it would be better to do *b*?

If akratic action does not arise from deliberation but is merely inconsistent with one's better judgement, it starts to lose its notes of strangeness. As outlined earlier (Section 3.1), arguments for the possibility of akratic action proceed by constructing an architecture of practical judgement which allows for deliberation over what to do giving rise to actions divergent with one's better judgement. Such talk is naturally heard as concerning the nature of *deliberation over what to do*.

Arpaly has it that the prescription to act against one's better judgement is 'flagrantly absurd', and so doing so cannot result from deliberation. For me, this is precisely what's interesting about akrasia. In seeking to make some akratic action rational, Arpaly takes action of this kind out of the deliberative realm. As a broader picture of the space of possibilities regarding rational action, non-deliberative action may well take its place. But acting *inconsistently with* one's better judgement is not always to act *against* one's better judgement. Thus, in conceiving of akratic action as a member of the class of non-deliberative actions, we may have changed the subject.

3.3 Concluding Remarks

Notwithstanding notable exceptions, there is consensus that cases of akratic action are those performed *against one's better judgement*. We have seen that this is something which, with some creative modelling of the cognitive architecture, can be rendered possible, but irrational. Although often held up as a paradigm case of irrationality, such irrationality consists in failing to have one's action guided by one's best judgement, and that failure is attributed to a variety of causes, none unique to akrasia. And, in fact, there are ripples of dissent concerning whether akratic action is irrational after all. If we allow for a broader view of rational action, not taking it to consist solely in one's practical judgements being appropriately related to one's better judgement, we see that there are some cases where that appropriate relation does not hold, but where we might reasonably deny irrationality. Or, if we take akratic action not to be the output of faulty deliberation concerning what one should do, but rather as non-deliberative, we are welcome, as in the epistemic case of belief change via dawning, to see some cases as rational after all.

4 Strange Belief

Strange beliefs are perhaps the most obvious cases of irrationality. We saw earlier (Section 2.2) that belief is thought to be subject to several rationality constraints, and we mentioned consistency, inferential coherence, and standing in an appropriate relationship to evidence. Let us say a little more about these ideas.

It is commonplace to take *consistency* to rationally constrain beliefs, which is to say, rationality requires that we do not hold inconsistent beliefs. Understood in the strictest sense, as requiring that we hold *no* inconsistent beliefs, this is probably too demanding. As Spaulding (2015) points out, 'we have innumerable beliefs, and it is very likely that lots of them are inconsistent with each other' (471). An easy way to see this is to get creative and take advantage of mistaken identities generating inconsistent beliefs. Having never met Ruth, my (philosophical) hero (as per the advice), and having little clue as to what she looks like, I have a longstanding belief that she is generous and kind. At a conference I meet a very rude philosopher over dinner, who I believe to be ungenerous and unkind. That philosopher, unbeknownst to me, is my philosophical hero Ruth. I have inconsistent beliefs in this case (I believe that *Ruth is kind and generous*, and that *Ruth is ungenerous and unkind*),[14] and so fail the rationality constraint on its strictest reading.

A more sensible way to understand the demands of consistency is as requiring the appropriate revision of belief when one is aware of inconsistency. If after the conference dinner I tell a colleague about the ungenerous and unkind philosopher I was unfortunate enough to sit next to, and my colleague replies 'But Ema,

[14] I've taken advantage of the *de dicto* ('about what is said') sense of my belief that *Ruth is generous and kind*, and the de re ('about the thing') sense of my belief that *Ruth is ungenerous and unkind*. (A similar mischievousness can quickly generate the result that one knowingly falsely believes (Crimmins 1992)). Conceiving of the rationality constraint of consistency in the strictest terms doesn't allow us to distinguish cases like this from cases of more explicit endorsement of inconsistent contents.

that's *Ruth*!' then rationality demands of me that I reject one of the beliefs forming the inconsistent set. I must either reject my belief that *Ruth (my philosophical hero) is generous and kind* (perhaps I had mistakenly taken these qualities to follow from philosophical excellence). Or I must reject my belief that *Ruth (my dinner companion) is ungenerous and unkind* (perhaps she's just tired and irritable after a long day). Of course, I may not know in that moment which of those beliefs to reject, and rationality would demand too much to insist that I choose immediately, not least because 'there may be more pressing epistemic tasks to carry out, which it would be correspondingly irrational to set to one side' (Bermúdez 2001: 465). So long as I feel the incoherence and recognise that something has to give, I count as a rational believer.[15]

Let us turn to inferential coherence, the idea that one should believe that which follows from beliefs already held. If I believe that *my son has had too much sugar today*, and I believe that *when my son has had too much sugar he sleeps badly*, I should also believe that *my son will sleep badly*. As with the consistency constraint, taking it at its strictest may not deliver us the most plausible evaluations of rationality. In giving my son his second scoop of ice cream, I may well believe that *he has had too much sugar today*, but given his excellent run of sleeping recently, and his generally low sugar consumption, my belief that *when my son has had too much sugar he sleeps badly* isn't at the front of my mind. We might forgive my failing to infer that *my son will sleep badly*; inference sometimes eludes us when we're forgetful or distracted, and us being so may, of course, render the constituents of an inferential relation less salient. Let us suppose though that upon spotting my son hungrily enjoying his second scoop, a friend reminds me that sugar interferes with his sleep. Now my long-standing belief that *when my son has had too much sugar he sleeps badly* strikes me. And *now* I am criticisable if I fail to draw the inference and believe that *my son will sleep badly* – all else being equal, rationality requires that I form this belief.

[15] Some pressure on even this weaker requirement comes from the *paradox of the preface*, first introduced by David C. Makinson (1965). When an author at the start of their book thanks helpful colleagues, following up with 'although any errors are mine', they're making sure that they pre-emptively exonerate their helpful colleagues from blame in the event that errors are discovered, but they're also indicating that they hold inconsistent beliefs. On the one hand the author presumably believes all the various claims asserted in the book although (although see Leitgeb 2014), and thus, believes that there are no errors. On the other hand, their declaration in the preface suggests that they *at the same time* believe that there are errors (or at least, that there might be). We might take the preface declaration 'to present a living and everyday example of a situation which philosophers have commonly dismissed as absurd; that it is sometimes rational to hold logically incompatible beliefs' (Makinson 1965: 205).

Our final rationality constraint was that our beliefs should stand in an appropriate relationship to evidence, which is to say, they should be formed on the basis of sufficient evidence and be revisable in the face of counterevidence.[16] Very often, when beliefs are deemed irrational, it is in virtue of their failing to be properly related to evidence. That's certainly true for the kinds of belief we'll discuss in this section, where being formed on the basis of poor evidence, and/or being irresponsive to counterevidence is sometimes even taken to be definitional of those kinds.

Both ways of a belief being related to evidence (*formed* on the basis of and *revisable* in response to) are important for rationality. I might have excellent evidence for my belief that *my neighbour owns a dog* – I hear its incessant barking, I see my neighbour walking it most days, her returning from the pet shop with dog food, and so on. So far, so rational. But if my neighbour tells me that she's dog sitting this week for her sister to whom the dog belongs, I had better revise my belief that *my neighbour owns a dog*. If I fail to revise the belief upon sufficient counterevidence, my belief is irrational.

Equally, suppose that I believe that *my neighbour owns a dog*, and *if* my neighbour were to present me with sufficient counterevidence for my belief (e.g. if she told me that she was dog sitting for her sister), I *would* revise my belief. But now suppose that the reason I believe that *my neighbour owns a dog* in the first place is because I had a dream that she did, or perhaps I simply had a knock to the head which generated that belief in me. My belief's being revisable in response to counterevidence does not by itself mean that it holds the right relationship to evidence – it needs to have been formed on the basis of good evidence in the first place.

We have a sense now, I hope, of the rationality constraints on belief. Before turning to our cases of interest, I speak briefly to something which might otherwise become an elephant on the page – whether our cases are ones of *belief* at all.

4.1 Doxasticism about Strange Belief

The commonality among the beliefs we will consider is that they all look a bit different from ordinary belief. Some philosophers have found these differences so compelling that they have argued that we are not in the domain of irrational belief

[16] Some folk take the appropriate relationship to evidence to be not a mark of *rational* belief, but rather, a mark of belief *simpliciter*. Carolina Flores notes that the 'orthodox view in philosophy is that belief is *constitutively* evidence-responsive' (Flores *forthcoming*, my emphasis). This doesn't mean that, for example, all beliefs necessarily respond to counterevidence. Rather the thought is that in believing that *p*, a subject '*has the capacity* to respond to evidence bearing on the belief that *p* by rationally updating their belief that *p*' (Flores *forthcoming*, my emphasis). See Grace Helton (2018) for a defence of this view.

after all, and that is because we are not in the domain of *belief*! *Doxasticism* about a given attitude type is the view that tokens of that attitude type are *beliefs*. *Non-doxasticism* about a given attitude type is the view that tokens of that attitude type are *not beliefs*. Non-doxasticists will often pair this negative claim with a positive one about how we should understand the attitude instead. That is, once the attitude type is cast out of the belief club, non-doxasticists will sign it up for membership to a different club, perhaps the club of *imagination*, or mere *avowal*.

Non-doxasticism about the cases to be considered later in the Element is typically motivated by characterising *all* beliefs (not just the rational ones) as, necessarily, having certain features. This might relate to their formation and revision (e.g. appropriate relationship to evidence), or to their downstream effects (e.g. that in concert with appropriate desires, beliefs *motivate action*). When attitudes fail to be formed or revised in line with these constitutive constraints, or when they fail to motivate the kind of action one would expect from a belief with a given content, it thus follows that those attitudes are not beliefs after all. Broadly speaking, when doxasticists seek to keep the target attitude in the club of belief, they have pursued two options. They will either loosen strict conceptions of belief on the grounds that a whole host of attitudes we standardly take to be beliefs also fail along some dimension of such strict conceptions, or they will argue that the target attitude has the features required of the strict conceptions after all.

Whether attitudes arising from conspiratorial ideation, self-deception, and delusion are beliefs matters for the project pursued in this section. That's because what we are able to say about the rationality of any given attitude will depend on what kind of attitude it is. For example, some non-doxasticists appeal to *imagination* to model their target attitudes.[17] Whether an attitude is a belief or an imagining has clear implications for what can be said about whether or not it is rational. Consider Nikki and Sebastian, who both have an attitude with the content *there's a duck hiding in my office*. They arrive at their respective offices one morning and spot a feather on the floor. This prompts Nikki to *believe* that *there's a duck hiding in my office*, whilst it prompts Sebastian to merely *imagine* that *there's a duck hiding in my office*. We can see that the contents of Nikki's and Sebastian's attitudes are the same, and we've even specified that they are prompted by the same event – perceiving a feather on their office floors. But neither of these things, singularly or combined, will settle the matter as to whether Nikki's and Sebastian's attitudes are *rational* (or not). We probably want to say that Nikki's attitude is *irrational*. Why? In so believing, Nikki may have violated rationality constraints on belief. Perhaps her

[17] Gregory Currie (2000) has argued that delusions are not beliefs but imaginings that the subject misidentifies as beliefs. Anna Ichino (2024; 2020) has argued for an imagination view of religious attitudes and has suggested that the imagination may be a better candidate for modelling superstitious attitudes.

belief is inconsistent with other beliefs she has, for example, that *there aren't any ducks on campus*, or that *ducks are never properly described as 'hiding'*. Or perhaps she ought to have inferred that there is not a duck in her office given that that follows[18] from her beliefs that *she locked her office door* and *ducks can't pick locks*. At the very least the evidence for her belief is insufficient, particularly as her office is not situated in a duck-dense environment. What about Sebastian? We probably don't want to say that his attitude is *irrational*. Why not? To do so would make epistemology particularly stuffy. Surely Sebastian is free to smile to himself and allow the presence of the feather to prompt a fun imagining of a duck hiding in his office (this might be an instrumentally irrational thing to allow if it distracts him from his work all day, or if he has a duck phobia, but for a judgement of irrationality to stand up, we'd need to be creative in stipulating further features of the broader context).

In evaluating our attitudes with respect to rationality then, we are engaged in a project downstream of settling what kind of attitude we're talking about. To keep things manageable, I will presume doxasticism throughout (and will refer readers to non-doxastic approaches). This will allow us to keep the goal posts stationary. Non-doxasticists are entitled to assess these attitudes as irrational (or not), but their case for such assessments will be very different from the parallel cases generated when working with a background presumption of doxasticism.

4.2 Belief and Bias

Before turning to our cases of interest, we need to say something about *bias*, since often it is by appeal to biases that philosophers and psychologists have explained the formation and maintenance of the beliefs we will discuss. To say that someone's reasoning exhibits a *bias*, we need to have in mind what that bias is a deviation *from*. For our purposes, we can have in mind the Standard Picture noted earlier (Section 2.2), where we understood rationality as reasoning in line with principles based in the rules of logic, probability theory, and so on. To say of someone's belief that it was formed or maintained in a biased way, is to say of it that it was formed or maintained in a way which departs from ideal belief formation and maintenance practices, and that it does so *along a particular dimension*.[19]

---

[18] Putting aside the possibility of human lock-picking duck depositors.

[19] We might model *ideal belief formation* (at least insofar as it relates to the processing of evidence) using Bayes' Theorem, which has it that: $P(h/e) = P(e/h) \cdot P(h)/P(e)$
Where 'P' is probability, 'h' is the hypothesis one is deliberating about, and 'e' is the evidence in favour of the hypothesis. It might be thought that ideal rationality demands that one processes evidence and updates one's belief (or at least one's *confidence*) in line with this. On the other hand, nothing in this approach prevents 'bonkers prior beliefs and loopy likelihood functions', which undermines the idea that Bayesian reasoning is rational reasoning (Coppock 2022: 123). In any case, it is enough for our purposes to have a rough idea in mind of what it is to

Suppose I wanted to explain the presence of *philosophical beliefs*, or a subset of them, perhaps what Marga Reimer has labelled *nihilistic philosophical doctrines*. These might include external world scepticism, hard determinism about free will, and anti-realism about morality (Reimer 2010: 317). Now let us (perhaps implausibly) imagine that we take the endorsement of nihilistic philosophical doctrines to call for explanation, perhaps because there are a host of other (more mainstream) philosophical doctrines on the market that are more explanatorily fruitful and less gloomy. What we might do is take some nihilistic philosophers as our experimental group, and some non-nihilistic philosophers as our control group. We could then design an experiment which tests for reasoning biases outside of the philosophical context. Perhaps we'd ask our philosophers to select their preferred explanation for a range of imaginary events, where those explanations were subject to variables like *plausibility* or *pessimism*. If we found that nihilistic philosophers were more likely to opt for explanations which scored highly on our variable of *pessimism*, we would have evidence for the claim that nihilistic philosophers exhibited the *pessimism bias*.[20] Attributing the *pessimism bias* to nihilistic philosophers would then be (at least part of) the explanation for why they endorse nihilistic philosophical doctrines over sunnier alternatives. This is (very roughly) how much of the psychological research on strange beliefs has proceeded, and we'll discuss some of it in the following section.

One more point before we go on: it is useful to distinguish *cold* from *hot* biases. Cold biases are non-motivational and emerge from heuristics, whilst hot biases are those driven by emotions and desires. Examples of the former are the availability bias (our tendency to rely on examples which easily come to mind as representative), and the confirmation bias (our tendency to search for or interpret information that confirms our existing beliefs). Hot biases are those arising from motivation, most obviously, our desiring that *p* or our desiring to *believe that p*. This desire might, for example, bias the evidence we gather or the evidence we attend to.[21] Let us turn now to our three cases of strange belief.

appropriately respond to evidence and counterevidence. We needn't mathematically model appropriate evidence processing in order to support the idea that our target attitudes are going wrong in this regard.

[20] A real experiment of this kind would, of course, need to consider other interpretations, for example that nihilistic philosophers exhibited unrealistic optimism to a lesser degree than non-nihilistic philosophers.

[21] Throughout this section I discuss the idea that motivated reasoning plays a role in the formation and maintenance of strange beliefs. However, the idea that cognition can be motivationally driven is contested. Alexander Coppock (2022) has argued instead that people are persuaded (if only a little) in the direction of information when they encounter it, and that 'people from different groups respond to persuasive information in the same direction and by about the same amount' (3). This approach contrasts rather clearly with a framework which seeks to explain apparent differences in how people respond to information by appeal to hypothesised motivations.

4.3 Conspiracy Beliefs

The term *conspiracy theory* can be understood to pick out an explanation of an event that appeals to the intentional states of conspirators, who intended the event and kept their intentions and actions secret (Mandik 2007: 206). So far, so epistemically respectable, after all, some conspiracy theories are true, well justified, and so on. Most of us believe that *Guy Fawkes conspired to blow up Parliament in 1605 with assistance from a handful of co-conspirators and thirty-six barrels of gunpowder.* But discussion of *that* belief doesn't belong in a book about irrationality, and endorsement of *that* belief doesn't make one a *conspiracy theorist*, as that term is standardly used.[22] These are not the conspiracy theories which will interest us here.

The theoretical interest in conspiracy theories arises not just from their contents, but also from their being held in opposition to some received view or orthodoxy. The reason one doesn't have to be a *conspiracy theorist* to endorse the Guy Fawkes conspiracy theory, is that doing so puts one in good company (that of the relevant epistemic authorities, in this case, historians). This is why some philosophers have defined conspiracy theories in a way that makes this feature explicit. To give just two examples of a more general trend: David Coady (2003) argues that 'the proposed explanation must conflict with an "official" explanation of the same historical event' (201) and Ichino and Juha Räikkä (2021) have it that the explanation 'conflicts with the received explanation of the said event, providing an alternative to the "official view" of that event' (249). I'll follow these authors and understand the phenomenon of interest to be those beliefs in theories concerning conspiracies which are in conflict with official explanations of events. I'll use the term *conspiracy belief* to pick out belief in such theories.[23]

Let us introduce some examples. Jack believes that *NASA and governments worldwide are covering up the fact that the Earth is flat.* Joe believes that *Covid-19 is a side effect of 5G towers.* Romany believes that *the*

[22] A more neutral use of the term *conspiracy theory* has been defended M. R. X. Dentith (2018) who argues for particularism about conspiracy theories, that is, when it comes to whether a conspiracy theory is rational or not, we must judge it on its merits (330). Something's merely being a conspiracy theory, contrary to the opposing *generalist* approach, doesn't yet tell us anything about its rational status (although see Noordhof *manuscript*). My discussion will have a generalist bent, but that's an artefact of my interest being only in epistemically problematic conspiracy beliefs.

[23] Non-doxastic approaches to conspiracy attitudes are so far few in number. One example is Ichino and Räikkä (2021), who give some reasons to think that at least some conspiracy theorists should be understood not as *believing* conspiracies, but as merely *hoping* the endorsed conspiracy is true, or as merely *communicating support* for the creators and supporters of conspiracy theories (248). Ichino and Räikkä, though, are relatively modest, not going as far as endorsing non-doxasticism, but only suggesting that non-doxastic approaches 'deserve serious attention' (238).

'terrorist attacks' on the Twin Towers in New York City and the Pentagon in Washington were an inside job. One interesting feature of conspiratorial ideation is that believing in one conspiracy theory is highly predictive of believing in others, indeed, 'the single best predictor of belief in one conspiracy theory is belief in a different conspiracy theory' (van Prooijen and Douglas 2018: 898). Several explanations of this have been proposed, ranging from a broader underlying belief which supports the endorsement of conspiracy theories in general (Wood, Douglas, and Sutton 2012), to various cognitive contributions (discussed in what follows) which characterise the conspiracy theorists' reasoning, which might make attractive multiple conspiracy theories.

A related point is that conspiracy theorists may feel the burden of the rationality constraint of consistency,[24] in such a way that their conspiracy beliefs become more elaborated. Often, for consistency, one has to accept further conspiracy theories in order to maintain existing ones. For example, if you believe that *NASA and governments worldwide are covering up the fact that the Earth is flat*, you'll also have to believe that *the moon landings were faked* and that *aircraft pilots and scientists are involved in the cover-up*, and so on. From one belief, others sometimes must grow, otherwise the initial theory becomes unstable.

Conspiracy theories may mutually support one another, but they are all in conflict with received wisdom from the relevant epistemic authorities. So how do people end up with them? A huge amount of research in cognitive and social psychology has sought to answer this question, of which we can only scratch the surface. The first thing to note is that, despite many conspiracy beliefs being extremely strange in their contents, they are taken by most researchers to be a 'normal' phenomenon (Pierre 2020: 618). So, when researchers try to understand why, for example, Jack believes the flat Earth conspiracy, they're not trying to identify unique irrationalities or pathologies in the way he forms and maintains his beliefs. Rather, they're looking to identify particular normal range features of cognition or social position which contribute to the endorsement of conspiracy theories. As Joe Pierre (2020) puts it with respect to the former:

[24] Although there is some evidence that conspiracy theorists endorse inconsistent conspiracy theories (see e.g. Wood, Douglas, and Sutton 2012; compare van Prooijen et al. 2023). Michael Wood, Karen Douglas, and Robbie Sutton take this to be evidence that the association of conspiracy beliefs with one another is driven by 'the coherence of each theory with higher-order beliefs that support the idea of conspiracy in general' (771), which is to say, a more general belief about, for example, *the likely deceptive operating of authorities* would encourage endorsement of multiple (even inconsistent) conspiracy theories.

> [M]any of the cognitive biases and other psychological quirks that have been found to be associated with belief in conspiracy theories are universal, continuously distributed traits varying in quantity as opposed to all-or-none variables or distinct symptoms of mental illness. (618)

Let us turn now to a discussion of the rationality of conspiracy beliefs.

4.3.1 Conspiracy Beliefs and (Ir)rationality

Beginning with rationality constraints on belief, the most obvious one violated by conspiracy theorists is the proper processing of evidence. When we say that someone is forming beliefs in a biased way, often what we mean is that the way in which they respond to evidence is biased, giving more weight to evidence supporting the kind of explanation which is favoured, and less to evidence opposing it. The cognitive biases attributed to those who have conspiracy beliefs are ones which influence the processing of evidence. Let us turn to those now.

One suggestion is the *intentionality bias*, which leads us to favour explanations which cast intentional agents in a key role, that is, events are attributed to the intentions and actions of conspirers, over mere accident, coincidence, or mechanical cause (i.e. a preference for *conspiracy* over *cock-up*) (see e.g. Brotherton and French 2015; Douglas et al. 2016). After much investigation, the origins of COVID-19 are not yet determined, with the front-running hypotheses being that it originated from a food market, with possible bat origins, or from an accidental lab leak. Neither of these hypotheses would satisfy a mind skewed by the intentionality bias, since neither hypothesis centres the intentional actions of human agents. Evidence for these hypotheses then may well be given rather short shrift. On the other hand, the hypothesis that COVID-19 was intentionally produced might strike someone whose reasoning exhibited the intentionality bias to be more plausible. Evidence for this hypothesis may well be diligently attended to.

A nearby suggestion is that the *proportionality bias* plays a role, according to which ‘when big things happen, we look for big causes’ (Brotherton 2015: 211). Causes that we take to be *big* in the relevant respect are those that involve the actions of intentional and powerful agents (Ebel-Lam et al. 2010; Leman and Cinnirella 2007). The hypothesis that COVID-19 was an *accident* of some kind will not satisfy a desire for a cause as *big* as the event which we’re seeking to explain, and evidence for the hypothesis may not sway a subject prone to proportionality bias. An international pandemic responsible for an excess mortality of at least 14.9 million (as of the end of 2021) (WHO 2023) might be thought to demand an explanation of similar magnitude.

A slightly different suggestion is the *causality bias*, which inclines subjects to posit meaningful causal connections between events (van der Wal et al. 2018). If Mike believes that *vaccines cause autism*, he'll put great stock in the fact that some children are vaccinated and later diagnosed with autism (taking this as evidence for his belief), even if relative rates of autism among vaccinated and unvaccinated children are the same. Many other features have been identified that might prompt conspiratorial ideation, including other cognitive biases, as well as motivational, social, and environmental factors (for an overview see Douglas and Sutton 2023).

We can also think about how conspiracy beliefs are maintained. It is one thing to form a conspiracy belief on flimsy evidence, but it's quite another to maintain that belief in the light of significant counterevidence. Of course, the biases which helped prompt the belief may have a role to play – if the proportionality bias led me to prefer the hypothesis that COVID-19 was intentionally produced and released as a bioweapon, it might also lead me to undervalue evidence for the alternative explanation casting the profoundly significant international pandemic as a mere unfortunate twist of nature. That explanation just doesn't satisfy me if I think or feel that big events need big explanations, and so the evidence in its favour may not be given its due.

Evidence-resistance has been taken to be central to conspiracy beliefs, with conspiracy theorists' hasty dismissal of counterevidence described as 'arguably the most important feature of conspiracy theories' (McKenna 2017: 57; see also Napolitano 2021: 83). Although the cognitive biases proposed to be involved with the formation of conspiracy beliefs may also be put to work in explaining belief maintenance, there are in addition, other, more social phenomena which are instructive.

Epistemic bubble is the term given to one's bespoke social epistemic structure, in which some points of view are excluded (Nguyen 2020: 142). Consider Kathleen, a British citizen who is a member of the Labour Party. In her online social networks, she rarely sees content from, for example, Conservatives, because folk who believe in conservatism are not well represented in her social groups, which largely determine her overall epistemic environment. Now consider Joe, our COVID-19 conspiracy theorist. He also inhabits an epistemic bubble, though one very different from Kathleen's. Indeed, it is rare that he would see content from the scientific community, and it is common for him to see content relating to purported rates of side effects and fatalities from vaccines, data on the respective locations of 5G towers and higher COVID rates, and so on. Epistemic bubbles are epistemically unideal – as by-products of our social environments they set the boundaries on the kind of information we are exposed to. However, there is a more epistemically pernicious kind of phenomenon which may be implicated in the maintenance of conspiracy beliefs.

Echo chamber is a term which picks out a social epistemic structure which makes itself *invulnerable* to opposing points of view, because they are pre-emptively discredited (Nguyen 2020: 142). Echo chambers might be thought more concerning from an epistemic point of view because they are *self-sealing*.[25] This can be achieved through what Endre Begby (2021) has called *evidential pre-emption*. This occurs

> when a speaker, in addition to offering testimony that *p*, also warns the hearer of the likelihood that she will subsequently be confronted with apparently contrary evidence: this is done, howsoever, not so as to encourage the hearer to temper her confidence in *p* in anticipation of that evidence, but rather to suggest that the (apparently) contrary evidence is in fact misleading evidence or evidence that has already been taken into account. (515)

Suppose now that Kathleen and Joe inhabit echo chambers. In Kathleen's case, if her left-leaning echo chamber is any good, it will self-seal against Conservative politicians singing the praises of one of their new policies – Kathleen will discredit the praise, not on its merit, but *because* it comes from the mouth of a Conservative politician who is thus probably lying and out for themselves. Joe's echo chamber, if it's any good, will self-seal against epidemiologists warning of the dangers of not getting vaccinated, because those are precisely the people who stand to benefit from lying to the populace about vaccines. For Kathleen and Joe, the Conservative politician and the epidemiologist are unlikely to break through – their testimonies have been *evidentially pre-empted*. If someone enchambered is exposed to information from the opposing side, they already have the tools and the psychological disposition to discredit it. Echo chambers then can help explain the evidence resistance of conspiracy beliefs, because counterevidence is pre-emptively dismissed.

The role of one's epistemic environment is clearly and obviously crucial to the formation and maintenance of conspiracy beliefs. Indeed, recently it has been argued that it is key to a proper assessment of such beliefs, generating the perhaps surprising result that conspiracy beliefs are *rational*. Let us turn now to Neil Levy's defence of this claim. Levy is interested in *bad beliefs*, understood as those which are *unjustified*, which conflict with the beliefs held by the *relevant epistemic authorities*, and which are maintained in the face of public availability of evidence in favour of more accurate beliefs, or in the face of

[25] Jennifer Lackey (2021) has argued that echo chambers considered simply as epistemic structures are not epistemically problematic; it is only when an echo chamber forms an *unreliable* epistemic structure that a problem arises.

knowledge that the relevant epistemic authorities have these more accurate beliefs. Conspiracy beliefs are the most obvious fit for such a category. Levy argues that conspiracy beliefs are the products of entirely *rational* processes, formed as a result of appropriately responding to evidence. What is going wrong in these cases is that the epistemic environment abounds with misleading evidence. We have perfectly rational belief formation operating in response to an epistemically polluted landscape (Levy 2021: xiii).

Consider again Joe, who finds himself in various epistemic bubbles and echo chambers which both initially prompt, and help to maintain, his belief that *COVID-19 is a side effect of 5G towers*. Those critical of Joe with respect to the rationality of his belief might grant that his evidence base is largely constituted by sources that support his conspiracy belief, but they may also point out that he ought to be able to distinguish good and bad evidence, recognise relevant experts, and defer appropriately. Perhaps being able to identify epistemic authorities and afford them due epistemic weight is part of what it is to be a rational believer in an epistemic environment teeming with disagreement. Levy (2021) takes this to be far too demanding, arguing that being able to distinguish reliable from unreliable sources of evidence is simply 'too difficult for ordinary people to reasonably be expected to accomplish' (117; see Murphy-Hollies and Caporuscio 2023 in reply). Our epistemic environments are extremely *polluted*, and distinguishing novices from experts on a given topic is incredibly difficult, particularly as the markers we might use to come to these judgements (credentials, track record, etc.) may not help us do so, since one of the constituents of epistemic pollution is the mimicry of such markers (Levy 2021: 112).

For those of us (hello reader!), who take ourselves to do quite well epistemically, Levy has it that our success is due to our being embedded in the right epistemic networks and our deferring to the right epistemic authorities. Now it is one thing to excuse conspiracy theorists for their beliefs by reference to their poor epistemic environments and their failing to defer to the right sources, but that's not yet to claim that such believers are forming and updating their beliefs *rationally*. How does Levy make good on this surprising claim? The idea is that the reasoning processes which promote success in folk embedded in the right epistemic networks, are the same processes which lead to conspiracy beliefs for those in more polluted and unideal epistemic environments. What we're all doing – far more often than is realised – is *rationally deferring*: 'For much of what we know about the world, we are deeply dependent on others' (Levy 2021: 50). Levy is highly pessimistic of the epistemic powers of individuals ('Alone we understand nothing' (59)), and argues that we thus outsource belief production, relying on others to maintain our beliefs across a range of domains. That's just as true of scientists (who 'use tools they didn't develop [...] often applied to data they didn't gather and which they can't verify, to test hypotheses that are constrained by theories they may not grasp' (Levy 2021: 54)), as it is of conspiracy theorists. And this deference is *rational* across the board.

Levy is arguing against approaches in epistemology which evaluate *individual* cognition, most obviously virtue epistemology, which does so within a framework of individuals' epistemic virtues and vices. Whilst we might be inclined to say that Kathleen exhibits the epistemic virtues of humility, due deference, objectivity, and so on in forming her beliefs, we might say of Joe that his conspiracy beliefs result from epistemic vices like closed-mindedness, naivety, and epistemic insouciance (indifference to whether one's beliefs are in good epistemic standing (Cassam 2018)). Levy has it that virtue epistemology can play only a limited role in guiding us towards better belief, or helping us to understand the formation of bad beliefs, and that's because epistemic virtues can only deliver epistemic goods in the appropriate environments (Levy 2021: 90). Those of us who are not bad believers should not too readily pat ourselves on the back and thank a suite of intellectual virtues as the secret to our success. Rather, we do well *because we defer*, and because we are embedded in particular epistemic networks where such rational deference doesn't lead us astray.

Let us conclude our discussion of the (ir)rationality of conspiracy beliefs with three points made against Levy's approach (Williams 2023). First, we can accept that bad beliefs are acquired through processes of social learning (i.e. deference), but such learning is also vulnerable to irrationality (indeed, perhaps more so insofar as it is psychologically easier to dismiss testimony against one's favoured belief compared to dismissing evidence of one's senses) (Williams 2023: 825). Whilst Levy (2021) has it that it is, for example, rational for climate-denial Conservatives to distrust non-Conservatives, because outgroup members are more likely to engage in deception (84), Daniel Williams (2023) suggests this 'is a strange form of rationality' (826). Even if it is rational to give *less credence* to evidence from members of one's outgroup, 'how could this justify the wholesale dismissal of the overwhelming majority of scientists on the topic?' (826). The point generalises; for many bad beliefs, 'people routinely seem to exhibit a shocking absence of epistemic care, sophistication, and vigilance against manipulation' (826).

Williams's (2023) positive view is not (or not just) that conspiracy beliefs are epistemically irrational, it is also that they are, nonetheless, 'rational responses to incentives' (826; see also his 2021). In cases where the stakes are low for getting something wrong, non-epistemic goods related to one's social or material status may recommend epistemically irrational beliefs as overall rational to adopt. Williams (2023) argues that his view (the *incentives account of bad beliefs*) is preferable to Levy's view for three reasons. First, the incentives account has the resources to count as epistemically irrational 'the most extreme forms of racist, sexist, ethnocentric, and ultra-nationalist beliefs' that have taken centre stage in some groups, and would thus be recommended by Levy's rational deference (828). Second, the incentives account delivers the right result when we're thinking about some cases of dissent from the opinion of the majority (on Levy's view this would be irrational, but there are cases of consensus-disputing which we take to be epistemically rational). Finally, it has been shown that epistemic virtues are conducive to accurate belief formation – including within social learning – and interestingly, these are the kind of virtues absent from the epistemic conduct displayed by political partisans (Tetlock 2017, cited in Williams 2023: 829). These virtues, however, do not play a role in Levy's account. According to Williams's view, the absence of these virtues is precisely what we should expect if conspiracy beliefs are rational responses to incentives, rather than sincere attempts at forming true beliefs.

4.3.2 Summary Remarks

I have focused on those conspiracy beliefs which go against the received wisdom endorsed by epistemic authorities (thus hedging my bets on whether this is true of *all* conspiracy beliefs proper, or just a subset; see fn. 22). We have seen some ways in which beliefs of this kind fare badly when held up to the Standard Picture. Conspiracy beliefs are sometimes inconsistent with other beliefs (sometimes other *conspiracy* beliefs) the subject holds, and perhaps most characteristically, they are formed on the basis of poor evidence, and not revised in the light of counterevidence. We saw some reasons that this might be so – certain reasoning biases which can affect the proper processing of evidence might be at play, as well as particular social epistemic structures which can influence the kind of information one is exposed to, and the kind of information one would accept as evidence. On the other hand, considerations regarding the epistemic environment have been appealed to in the service of rationalising conspiracy beliefs – understanding them as formed via epistemically rational processes operating in an epistemically polluted environment. Rationalising conspiracy beliefs by appeal to deference to one's in-group isn't cost free; we saw how doing so could mean rationalising some fairly abhorrent beliefs of certain groups, ruling out rational dissent, and not giving the role of epistemic virtues in rational belief their due. An alternative approach granted the claim that conspiracy beliefs are epistemically irrational, but had it that they can also be understood as rational responses to social and material incentives.

We turn now to our second kind of strange belief, those arising from self-deception.

4.4 Self-Deception

The literature on self-deception is vast, and as we have seen so far, often even pinning down the phenomenon of interest can be a controversial exercise. Let us begin with three examples which reflect at least some consensus.

> Katie loves her wife Frankie and wants their relationship to work. Lately, Frankie has been returning home from work late, distracted, and seems uninterested in Katie. She has also started wearing perfume, working out, and using a second phone for late night whispered calls. Katie's friend Phil says that it's obvious that Frankie is having an affair, but Katie believes that *Frankie is faithful*.
>
> Eileen has recently taken up boxing, and is due to have her first competitive fight next week. Her opponent is Jean, who is county champion, and has an unbroken string of wins under her belt this season. Eileen knows that going into the ring believing what the evidence suggests (that *she will lose*) will ensure her defeat. She also knows that she'll fight harder and perhaps even win if she believes that *she will beat Jean*. Eileen believes that *she will beat Jean*.
>
> Aaron is desperately anxious that he has failed his entrance exam for Law School. He's never failed an exam, and he worked hard in preparation for the exam, completed the paper in good time, and, during the exam, felt that things were going well. Nevertheless, Aaron believes that *he has failed the exam*.

In these examples, we can see what Neil Van Leeuwen (2007) identifies as three 'strands of consensus' in the philosophical literature regarding what self-deception involves:

1. A motivational component
2. The presence of information which would justify a different belief
3. The output of a truth-evaluable cognitive attitude

Let us identify each of these components in our examples. First, we can understand the requirement of a *motivational component* as an evaluative attitude (most often a desire) towards the content about which the subject is deceived. We can see that for each of our self-deceptive attitudes, there is a desire related to the content of the resulting belief. Our cases look rather different in this regard, and that is no accident. Rather they exemplify three kinds of self-deception, which differ with respect to how the motivational component relates to the content of the self-deceptive belief. Katie's case is of the classic variety: *wishful* self-deception, in which the subject desires that p, and the self-deceptive belief matches the content of the desire – the subject believes that p. Eileen's case is different. Although she desires to beat Jean, her route to a belief with that content is a little more circuitous. She recognises that her beliefs about the matter will make a difference to whether she wins or loses, and the desire in play in her self-deception is not the desire that *p* but rather the desire that *she believes that p*. This is the slightly odder case of *wilful* self-deception. Things look very different for Aaron, where he ends up believing that which he desires *not* to obtain. Aaron desires that he has not failed the exam and ends up with the belief that he has in fact failed the exam. This has been called *dreadful* (Van Leeuwen 2007: 425) or *twisted* (Mele 2001: 4) self-deception.[26]

The second strand of consensus is that there is information available to our subjects which would justify a different belief. In all of our cases, we have described our subjects' evidence (were they to give it its proper due) as supporting the opposite of the belief that they self-deceptively come to hold. For Katie, the evidence of Frankie's likely infidelity is clear – Frankie is probably being unfaithful. For Eileen, the evidence of her likely defeat is also clear, it is very unlikely that she will beat county champion Jean, whose current form is good. For Aaron, the evidence strongly suggests that he has passed the exam – a fail would be the first on his academic record, and there are no reasons to think that his sustained excellence is about to come to an end. Notice that our subjects don't believe anything that is demonstrably false, or for which the evidence in support of it couldn't be explained in a way consistent with the self-deceptive belief. If Katie caught Frankie in an unambiguous act of infidelity, we wouldn't take her continued belief in Frankie's fidelity to be a case of self-deception, the kind to which we may all fall prey. Rather, self-deceptive belief relies on there being enough interpretative space that the evidence against the belief can be explained in a way that is nevertheless consistent with it.

The third strand of consensus is that the self-deceptive process ends in the generation of a *truth-evaluable cognitive attitude*. The specification of this component is loose enough to allow in non-doxastic theories of self-deception, which we have already put aside.[27] For us, then, we can take self-deception to result in a *belief* in the content towards which one is self-deceived. Katie *believes*

[26] Whilst Van Leeuwen (2007) takes cases of twisted self-deception to include a motivational component ('the content of the motivational element is the negation of the content of the product of self-deception' (425)), Alfred Mele (2001) takes such cases to 'threaten the [. . .] claim that all self-deception is motivated or has a motivated component' (4–5).

[27] Non-doxastic approaches have been defended by Sophie Archer (2013), Audi (1982), Tamar Gendler (2007), and Georges Rey (1988). Eric Funkhouser's (2005) view is non-doxastic insofar as the self-deceptive content is not believed by the subject. Rather, she believes *that she believes* that content. Self-deception then results in a belief, but it is a false second-order belief about the beliefs one has. For a defence of doxasticism about self-deception see Van Leeuwen (2007).

that *Frankie is faithful*, Eileen *believes* that *she will beat Jean*, and Aaron *believes* that *he has failed the exam*.

Let us turn now to the question of self-deception and (ir)rationality.

4.4.1 Self-Deception and (Ir)rationality

The first two of the preceding strands of consensus speak to the irrationality of self-deception. The first had a role for motivation in the formation of the self-deceptive belief. But of course, it is standardly thought that any desires one has regarding *p* do not represent reasons to form the belief that *p*, only evidential considerations can be *reasons* for belief (although see fn. 6). And so, in cases of self-deception we, *by definition*, have the inappropriate influence of motivation on belief. Relatedly, the second strand of consensus has it that the self-deceptive belief is deviant with respect to evidence. Van Leeuwen (2007) captures this as there being information available to the subject which would justify a different belief (422), whilst Mele (2009) appeals to cognitive peers:

> S's belief that *p* is motivatedly irrational if, if D (the evidence readily available to S during the process of acquiring the belief that *p*) were made readily available to S's impartial cognitive peers who engaged in at least as much reflection on *p* as S does (and this is at least a moderate amount of reflection), then those who would conclude that *p* is false would significantly outnumber those who would conclude that *p* is true. (60–1; compare Noordhof 2009: 63–4)

If it is right to define self-deception as involving a deviant relationship with evidence, the idea of it resulting in a belief that is rational is a non-starter, since we have taken the appropriate relationship to evidence to be a key rationality constraint on belief.

Further details concerning to what extent, and in what way, self-deceptive beliefs exhibit irrationality will depend on our background theory of the nature of self-deception. Indeed, we will see that some accounts fall out of line with the preceding broad consensus, and do not make good on the idea that self-deceptive beliefs are inappropriately related to evidence – they must locate the irrationality elsewhere. I turn now to two broad approaches to the architecture of self-deception (intentionalism and non-intentionalism) and will give an overview of what we can say about the irrationality of self-deceptive beliefs on these models.

For intentionalist views (also known as *agency views*), self-deception is a kind of action aimed at getting the agent to form a belief that, at the time of the intention, she takes to be false. We find the clearest analogy with interpersonal deception in the intentionalist approach. However, it has struck many folk that intending to get oneself to believe something one believes to be false is impossible.[28]

In light of this, intentionalists have appealed to temporal or psychological partitioning. Suppose I am self-deceived that *my son is a talented genius.* Intentionalism with temporal partitioning would have it that I arrange the world such that I will be tricked in the future, ensuring that I do not remember the arrangings. If I want to believe that *my son is a talented genius*, I'll ensure that I put his primary school certificates on the fridge door, leave his old excellent school reports lying around, and keep the more recent, underwhelming reports of his school performance hidden in a drawer. The oddness of self-deceptive beliefs would come not from the psychological mechanisms responsible for the resulting belief, but from the purposeful arranging of the environment to mislead those mechanisms. If we thought that my resulting belief in my son's genius was irrational, it wouldn't be because it was based on insufficient evidence, or improperly responsive to counterevidence – I had already fixed things in such a way that I would be immune to criticism from those quarters. Officer, I have simply responded to the evidence as it is presented to me. We might instead question my willingness to bring about a false belief in myself, and see my desire's role in the formation of the belief (by having me arrange the evidence) to be the site of irrationality. Intentionalism with temporal partitioning then breaks away from the picture of self-deception we sketched earlier. Instead, one's relationship with evidence is deviant, but only indirectly.[29]

Another kind of partitioning is psychological, which models self-deceivers as holding contradictory beliefs. I both believe that which is suggested by the evidence (*my son is intellectually average*), *and* I believe the content about which I am self-deceived (*my son is a talented genius*). Psychological partitioning involves the cognitive system responsible for the deception being hidden from the self-deceived agent, which leaves her free to have the self-deceptive belief that *p*, whilst the more evidentially supported belief that *not-p* is hidden from her consciousness. Or, for those intentionalists who do not think that the deceptive part of the architecture harbours the belief that not-*p*, at the very least it will harbour the unconscious intentions to form the self-deceptive belief. The irrationality of self-deception on such views might be thought to lie in the

[28] Bermúdez (2000) distinguishes three ways to understand the self-deceiver's intention (310), and uniting them is an intention 'to bring it about that one acquires a belief that one knows one would not have acquired in the absence of that intention' (312). This enables him to respond to the objection that intentionalist accounts of self-deception cast self-deceivers as doing something impossible (i.e. intending to believe something one takes to be false).

[29] Some philosophers have argued that cases like these are not cases of self-deception after all, because 'the agent comes to believe that [*p*] in a perfectly familiar way' (Scott-Kakures 1996: 41).

inconsistency across partitions, for example, I both believe that *my son is intellectually average* and I believe that *my son is a talented genius*.

What about non-intentionalist (or non-agency) approaches? Very roughly, a non-intentionalist has it that self-deception results from cognitive biases, and not from an intention to form a belief with a particular content.[30] As we saw with our discussion of conspiracy beliefs, when people talk about biases, we can understand them as claiming that a subject is engaging in reasoning which is biased away from that promoted by the Standard Picture, reasoning which moves one away from the proper application of logical rules, probability, and so on. A non-intentionalist about self-deception has exactly this kind of picture to call on when explaining why self-deceptive beliefs are irrational. For example, Mele has given detailed characterisations of the generation of a self-deceptive belief by appeal to both hot and cold biases.

On the hot side, there is not an *intention* to form the belief that *p*, but rather a *desire that p*, and there are myriad indirect ways that such a desire can influence a subject in forming the belief that *p*. Let us consider four (Mele 2001: 26–7):

1. *Negative misinterpretation*: the subject misinterprets evidence against the desired belief that *p*, either as not counting against *p*, or as not counting strongly against *p*. If Frankie keeps coming home from work late, Katie may interpret this *not* as evidence of Frankie's infidelity, but rather as explainable by appeal to Frankie's new enthusiasm for her job.
2. *Positive misinterpretation*. The subject misinterprets evidence as supporting the desired belief that *p*. Eileen reasons that since Jean has had an unbroken string of wins recently, she's 'due' a loss.
3. *Selective focusing/attending*. The subject doesn't properly attend to evidence against the desired belief but focuses instead on evidence for the desired belief. I don't attend to my son's recent school reports, but often find myself thinking back to primary school parents' evenings where his teacher would speak of his advanced reading skills.

[30] Two in-between views should be noted. David Livingstone-Smith (2014) pitches his adaptationist model as an alternative to intentionalism and non-intentionlism, whilst reaping the benefits of both. On his view, self-deception has a biological purpose – it is the job of a sub-personal mechanism to selectively prevent the organism's representational apparatus from performing its proper function of accurate representation. More recently, Quinn Hiroshi Gibson (2020) has argued that the self-deceiver engages in *intentional omission* in the shape of acquiescing to the self-deceptive belief once it has been formed (660). The intentional side of self-deception then is divorced from the process of belief formation, which Gibson takes to solve the key problem of intentionalist approaches, whilst assuaging the intuition that self-deception is something for which the agent is responsible.

4. *Selective evidence-gathering*. The subject overlooks evidence against the desired belief (even when that is more accessible) and searches out evidence for the desired belief (even when that means mounting quite the search). Eileen overlooks the huge evidence base suggesting Jean will win the fight (most obviously, her recent track record), and goes searching the video archives for Jean's losses, assuring herself that Jean is beatable.

On the cold side, we can follow Mele (2001: 28–9) in identifying three ways in which biases of this kind may facilitate self-deception:

1. *Vividness of information*. Information that is more *vivid* to a subject is given greater weight. What information is *vivid* for a subject will depend on her interests. In Katie's case, the (albeit infrequent) moments of attentiveness from Frankie will strike her, and she will attend to these as evidence for Frankie's fidelity.
2. *Availability heuristic*. As noted earlier, this heuristic leads us to rely on examples which come to mind as indicative of relative likelihood. For example, Eileen's daily deep dive into archive footage of Jean's past losses leads her to overestimate the chance of Jean losing their fight.
3. *Confirmation bias*. As noted earlier, this bias leads us to search for or interpret information that confirms our existing beliefs. When my son answers a question correctly on *University Challenge*, I take that as evidence for my belief that he is a talented genius, ignoring his underwhelming recent school report that I shoved in a drawer.

We can see how biases of both the hot and cold variety can prop up an assessment of self-deceptive beliefs as irrational. In the hot case, our desires illegitimately move us to an improper treatment of evidence. In the cold case, as Mele notes, 'although sources of biased belief can function independently of motivation, they may also be triggered and sustained by motivation in the production of a particular *motivationally* biased belief' (Mele 2001: 29). In some cases then, cold biases can serve the interests of one's motivation, in facilitating the formation or maintenance of a self-deceptive belief. In such cases, cold biases which usually serve us well as useful-if-not-foolproof heuristics, because of the influence of desire, are put to work in the production of an irrational belief by facilitating the improper treatment of evidence.[31]

[31] Mele (2001) argues that there are further mechanisms for motivationally biased belief, and he combines the ideas of James Friedrich (1993) and Yaacov Trope and Akiva Liberman (1996) into what he calls the *Friedrich–Trope–Liberman* (FTL) model (31). This model accommodates costs of error (rejecting something true/accepting something false) and confidence thresholds on belief (for details on how this model helps us understand mechanisms in self-deception, see Mele 2001: 31–49).

4.4.2 Summary Remarks

I began by identifying three features of self-deception upon which there is broad consensus. These features already got us to the judgement that we were in the domain of irrational belief. However, some approaches to self-deception, namely, intentionalist views, may have a hard time making good on that assessment if they appeal to temporal partitioning. Then our self-deceived subject simply responds to the evidence as it is presented to her (and as it was arranged by an earlier self with the intention to deceive). Intentionalist views with psychological partitioning have an easier time being in line with the irrationality claim – they might appeal to the subject holding inconsistent beliefs. Non-intentionalist approaches, much like work on conspiracy beliefs, draw on a range of cognitive biases, most obviously hot, but also those which are cold, but co-opted by desire. What unites all of the biases that contribute to the formation or maintenance of a self-deceptive belief is that they adjust the subject's relationship to evidence away from what is appropriate. We turn now to our final kind of strange belief – delusion.

4.5 Delusion

Let us begin by putting aside the folk use of the term *delusion*, the kind one might employ in casual conversation. For example, I might tell my partner that he's *delusional* if he believes that his football team will win a trophy this year. If you're Richard Dawkins (2006), you'll take anyone who believes in a religious deity to be properly characterised as *delusional*. These are not the uses of the term that will concern us here. Rather, I use the term *delusion* to pick out those strange beliefs of interest to psychiatry.

We can begin, as is common, with a definition of delusion drawn from the most recent *Diagnostic and Statistical Manual of Mental Disorders*. There delusions are described as:

> fixed beliefs that are not amenable to change in light of conflicting evidence. Their content may include a variety of themes (e.g. persecutory, referential, somatic, religious, grandiose) [. . .] Delusions are deemed bizarre if they are clearly implausible and not understandable to same-culture peers and do not derive from ordinary life experiences [. . .] The distinction between a delusion and a strongly held idea is sometimes difficult to make and depends in part on the degree of conviction with which the belief is held despite clear or reasonable contradictory evidence regarding its veracity. (*DSM-5* 2013: 87)

Concerns have been raised with almost all components of this characterisation, specifically, with respect to the claims that all delusions are *held despite clear or reasonable contradictory evidence*, and that all delusions are *beliefs*[32] (for an overview see Sullivan-Bissett 2024: 3–6). We won't worry about these issues with the diagnostic criteria except where they arise with respect to our discussion of irrationality. Let us turn instead to some examples.

- Glen believes that *his daughter has been replaced by an imposter* (Capgras delusion)
- Marilyn believes that *she has ceased existing* (Cotard delusion)
- India believes that *she has a second head* (perceptual delusional bicephaly)

Let us also distinguish two types of delusion: *monothematic* and *polythematic*. Monothematic delusions concern a single theme and occur 'in isolation in people whose beliefs are otherwise entirely unremarkable' (Coltheart et al. 2007: 642). Polythematic delusions are more often elaborated and occur in the context of mental disorder. The relationships between monothematicity and circumscription on the one hand, and polythematicity and elaboration on the other are not exceptionless (Davies et al. 2001: 135), but this has nevertheless been taken to be a useful way to carve up the landscape. I'll focus on *monothematic* delusions (our three examples fall into this category), because the debates which concern our question of rationality have taken place within this context.

One important feature of many monothematic delusions which is crucial for understanding their etiology is *anomalous experience*. For example, in the Capgras delusion, subjects experience a lack of affective response to somebody with whom they are close. In Cotard delusion, this lack of affective response may be generalised to the environment (Young et al. 1992: 200), or there is an experience of depersonalisation (see Gerrans 2024 for discussion of the Cotard experience). In perceptual delusional bicephaly, a subject may hallucinate a second head (see Ames 1984 for a case of this kind).

A common approach to understanding delusions is *empiricism*, which is the view that these anomalous experiences play a causal role in the formation and maintenance of delusions.[33] So, for example, the empiricist will say that Glen's

[32] Non-doxasticism about delusion has been defended by G. E. Berrios (1991), Currie (2000), Richard Dub (2017), and Andy Egan (2008). Keith Frankish (2009) has defended the view according to which delusions are *acceptances* (some of which are *second-order beliefs*, and some non-doxastic). For comprehensive defences of doxasticism about delusion see Bortolotti (2009) and Noordhof (2024a), and for critical discussion of non-doxastic approaches see Noordhof (2024b).

[33] I note two alternative approaches. Rationalism is the view that anomalous experience does not play a role in the formation of delusion. Rather, 'delusion is a matter of top-down disturbance in some fundamental beliefs of the subject, which may consequently affect experiences and actions' (Campbell 2001: 89; for critical discussion see Bayne and Pacherie 2004). Prediction-error theories have it that perceptual processing involves generating predictions about sensory input based on hypotheses about the world. These hypotheses are then updated in order to

lack of affective response when looking at his daughter is part of the explanation of why he believes that *his daughter has been replaced by an imposter*. India's hallucination of a second head is part of the explanation of why she believes that *she has a second head*. And so on. Broadly speaking, there are two ways of being an empiricist. *Explanationist approaches* understand delusions as *explanations of* anomalous experience, whilst *endorsement approaches* have it that the delusional content is present in the anomalous experience, and the subject *endorses* that content in her belief (Bayne and Pacherie 2004: 82). I'll talk in explanationist terms in what follows, since such an approach lends itself more straightforwardly to the ideas I discuss.

4.5.1 Delusion and (Ir)rationality

A natural way to think about delusion's irrationality is via the debate within empiricism over how many *factors* are involved in delusion. All empiricists agree that anomalous experience is one such factor. Where the disagreement lies is in whether we need to posit a second factor which characterises the belief formation or evaluation processes in people with delusions. One-factor theorists argue that we do not, two-factor theorists argue that we do.

Before proceeding, let us be very clear about what is meant by *factor*. In this debate, *factor* means more than mere *cause* (in my view, things go awry when this important point is not kept in view). Rather, a *factor* is a cause with the property of being *abnormal*. This is recognised by one- and two-factor theorists alike. For example, together with Paul Noordhof, I (2021) have defended a one-factor account. We understand a factor as 'an abnormality that explains the formation of abnormal beliefs' (10279). Two-factor theorists have said similar things. For example, Martin Davies, Aimola Davies, and Max Coltheart (2005) take the second factor to be 'a departure from what is normally the case' (228) and Tony Stone and Andrew Young (1997) talk of delusional reasoning being 'abnormal' and 'differences between people with and without delusion' (342). This makes sense; if we were in the business of mere *cause* we would need to appeal to many 'factors' because we would need to appeal to many causes. Rather, *factor*-talk allows us to identify the causes that are explanatorily relevant to *delusional* belief in particular.

minimise the error of these predictions on the basis of comparison between them and sensory input. Some prediction-error theories claim that delusions result from a malfunctioning of this process, whereby erroneous updating occurs and because of continuing faulty signals supporting the updated hypothesis, the delusion persists in the face of counterevidence (Corlett et al. 2010). Although prediction error theorists take their approach to be a competitor to two-factor approaches (insofar as they identify a single deficit, and also deny any sharp distinction between perceptual and doxastic mechanisms), some have argued that the two views need not be seen as rivals (see e.g. Miyazono, Bortolotti, and Broome 2014).

It might be thought that a one-factor account is a natural home for the claim that delusions are *rational*, whilst a two-factor account is well-placed to accommodate the, perhaps more plausible, claim that delusions are *irrational*. In fact, things are more nuanced. Let us begin by seeing if there's any mileage in the claim that delusions are *rational*.

Brendan Maher (the father of the one-factor approach) is often understood as claiming that forming a delusion on the basis of an anomalous experience is a *rational response* to that experience (e.g. Davies and Coltheart 2000: 8, Bentall et al. 2001: 1149, Bortolotti 2009: 47). There is one place in Maher's work where he makes a claim of this kind, suggesting that delusional hypotheses are 'rational *given the intensity of the experiences that they are developed to explain*' (1974: 104). However, taking Maher's body of work as a whole, that does not appear to be his considered view. Maher is interested not in *rationality* but in *normality*, having it that the cognitive activity of people with delusions is 'essentially indistinguishable' from that employed by non-delusional people, and talks of delusions being developed 'through the operation of *normal cognitive processes*' (1974: 103, my emphasis). Normal cognition, as this Element has shown, is home to a whole range of irrationalities, to which Maher is entitled in explaining the formation and maintenance of delusion. In addition, it has long been recognised that rationality is not the claim of the one-factor approach. Philip Gerrans (2002), drawing on Maher's work, notes that:

> one-[factor] accounts should not be thought of as claiming that a delusional subject is *rational* [. . .] Rather, the one-[factor] theorist should be understood as claiming that the actual psychology of belief formation, which departs considerably from ideal rationality, *functions in the same way in normal and delusional subjects*. (48, my emphasis)

This is not to say that a one-factor theory proper *cannot* claim that delusions are rational (see Noordhof and Sullivan-Bissett 2021: 10298–300 for a speculative attempt). Nevertheless, the real debate between one- and two-factor theorists does not concern the claim that delusions are irrational beliefs (that is granted on all sides), but rather concerns whether the irrationality of delusions is everyday, or something more substantial.

The irrationality of delusion might be thought to be demonstrable over and over again. Consider consistency. Some have suggested that to adopt a delusion is to adopt a belief inconsistent, or, at least, a belief which coheres badly, with one's other beliefs. For example, Brian McLaughlin (2009) has it that the Capgras delusion 'coheres very poorly' with many of the subject's background beliefs (143, see also Gerrans 2000: 114). McLaughlin doesn't say what these beliefs might be, but we can speculate that they include beliefs like *almost identical imposters aren't possible/likely, people don't/rarely get replaced, family and friends wouldn't systematically lie to me*, and so on. In forming the Capgras delusion, a subject forms a belief which at worst contradicts, and at best coheres poorly with, some of her other beliefs. Indeed, Coltheart and Davies (2021) have argued that the subject's conflicting knowledge or other beliefs ought to function as disconfirmatory evidence leading to the rejection of the delusional belief (222).

Delusions are also characterised in the DSM-5 as *evidence-resistant* beliefs, and Bermúdez (2001) identifies this feature as one shared by a variety of ways of characterising delusions (462). There are two sides to the coin here. On the one side, delusions are taken to be formed on evidence that does not properly support their 'wildly implausible' contents (Bortolotti and Broome 2008: 822), and on the other side, even if we could forgive the delusion's formation, we cannot forgive its being maintained in the face of clear counterevidence.

Finally, and relatedly, we can consider *hypothesis selection*. If delusions are explanations of anomalous experiences, why does the subject pick an explanation which is so spectacularly bad along dimensions of, for example, plausibility?[34] Surely, when Glen doesn't feel what he's used to feeling when he looks at his daughter, he shouldn't form the belief that *she is an imposter*! What about the belief that *he is tired* or *he is ill*, or even, *his daughter has changed her appearance in some way*? Those much more sensible beliefs might also explain Glen's strange experience.

Taking these points together then, we can now ask whether they get us to the claim that delusions are irrational in a way that is everyday, or in a way that is abnormal? Is the inconsistency or poor coherence with one's other beliefs a sign of an abnormally irrational mind? Does the subject with a delusion have an abnormal relationship with evidence, perhaps one inexcusably worse than normal subjects? Can a subject's opting for the delusional hypothesis over more epistemically respectable ones be laid at the door of normal range irrationality, or is there something more substantial going on?

The one-factor account will insist that the irrationality displayed is everyday. On consistency, the idea was that some delusions are inconsistent or cohere poorly with other beliefs one might hold, and the Capgras delusion has been offered as an example. However, it has been argued that this objection is overstated. For one thing, not only do we find Capgras themes in fiction, there are also news reports or rumours regarding people being replaced by look-alikes

[34] Others have gone further, arguing that not only are delusions poor explanations of anomalous experiences, they are 'nonstarters' and 'the explanations of the delusional patients are nothing like explanations as we understand them' (Fine et al. 2005: 160).

(Noordhof and Sullivan-Bissett 2021: 10299). In addition, delusional themes are often entrenched in a culture promoting background beliefs consistent with the delusion after all (Gold and Gold 2024). Finally, ordinarily irrational beliefs might be claimed to commit the sin of inconsistency or poor coherence (for an overview of the research demonstrating this see Bortolotti 2009: 78–87).

With respect to the relationship to evidence, it has been argued that the anomalous experiences function as a source of evidence for the delusion (Noordhof and Sullivan-Bissett 2021: 10280). It might be said in reply that even granting that the experience counts as evidence for the delusion (at least from the subject's point of view), it is easily outweighed by the evidence against the delusion. One-factor theorists have argued that this is to underappreciate the profundity of such experiences. As Maher (1988) put it, 'asking patients to prefer a naturalistic theory to their own' would be 'tantamount to asking them to trust the evidence of other people's senses in preference to their own' (25; see also Noordhof and Sullivan-Bissett 2021: 10297). Even granting, though, that the subject with a delusion has a shaky relationship with evidence – does this indicate an explanatory need for abnormal irrationality? One-factor theorists will say no – a whole host of beliefs are guilty of this. Indeed, Maher (1974) claimed that holding onto a belief in the face of counterevidence is something done by scientists (107) (philosophers too!), reluctant to let go of their pet theories. And, as we have seen, a poor relationship to evidence characterises a range of other beliefs, namely conspiracy belief and self-deceptive belief (among others). It is notable that these beliefs are not formed in response to highly anomalous experiences demanding an explanation. In addition, the adoption of the delusional hypothesis as an explanation for experience may bring both relief from anxiety and intellectual satisfaction, having now figured things out (Mishara 2010: 10). These may well be prizes normal subjects are loath to give up (Noordhof and Sullivan-Bissett 2021: 10297). For the one-factor theorist then, normal range irrationality can carry the day when it comes to accommodating the relationship between delusion and evidence.

Finally, what can be said about poor hypothesis selection? Perhaps two things. First, it is not just in the formation of *delusional* beliefs that subjects opt for implausible explanations over better ones. As we've seen, conspiracy theorists may well be equally accused (Section 4.3), so too might believers in the paranormal (Noordhof and Sullivan-Bissett 2023), and yet we are not tempted by the suggestion that we need anything beyond everyday irrationality to explain beliefs of these kinds. Of course, there are important differences between delusions and other irrational beliefs, but the latter do show us that poor hypothesis selection is not a charge that can be uniquely levelled at the former. In addition, once again, attending to the anomalous experiences often associated with delusions is instructive. Garry Young has argued that the Capgras subject may well feel 'justified in broadening the scope of what he feels is epistemically possible, as he looks to explain what is happening' (Young 2024: 161).[35] Indeed, even some two-factor theorists have not taken delusional hypothesis selection to be especially irrational, even arguing that it's Bayesian rational! For example, in the case of Capgras, Coltheart, Peter Menzies, and John Sutton (2010) argue that, on the basis of the abnormal data (they prefer talk of *data* over *experience*), it is Bayesian rational for a subject to form the imposter belief (that is, the Capgras delusion) (see McKay 2012).

Let us turn to two-factor accounts which take delusion to involve something more substantial than ordinary irrationality. The putative second factor might explain the various epistemic features of delusion we have been discussing. What distinguishes various two-factor accounts is the nature of the proposed second factor, and approaches can be distinguished as falling into one of three kinds: bias, deficit, or performance error.

We have seen bias accounts in the literature on conspiracy beliefs, although we noted in our discussion that the biases appealed to there were those found in the normal range. Normal range biases are of course something to which the one-factor theorist is also entitled to appeal, happily captured by Maher's talk of 'normal cognitive processes' (1974: 103). Thus two-factor theories positing a bias must understand that bias not to be operative in the normal range, or at the very least, to be a normal-range bias which is *exaggerated* in people with delusions. The bias exhibited by subjects with delusions on such accounts is not one that finds a home in everyday irrationality.

The role of the posited bias is to explain why the subject moves from the anomalous experience to the delusion. Two-factor theorists recognise the importance of anomalous experience, but they take the citing of a single abnormality to fall short of explaining the delusion.[36] The role of the bias is to bridge the explanatory gap left by the subject's moving from the experience to the delusion (rather than to another belief). Let us turn then to some of the biases proposed to do this work.

---

[35] We might also question the implicit assumption that alternative hypotheses are available to the subject forming a delusion (Sullivan-Bissett 2018: 938–40).

[36] Very often, two-factor theorists have motivated their view by construing the one-factor theory as committed to what I have elsewhere called *the sufficiency claim* (i.e. the claim that anomalous experience is *sufficient* for delusion formation). Apparent cases in the neuropsychological literature of subjects with the relevant anomalous experience but without the delusion thus straightforwardly falsify the one-factor account, so understood. However, the sufficiency claim has never been the claim of the one-factor account (Sullivan-Bissett 2020: 683, 2022: 2–4, Noordhof and Sullivan-Bissett 2021: 10281, 10282, 10297).

Perhaps the most famous suggestion is the *jumping to conclusions* bias, where subjects with delusions are said to require less evidence than subjects without delusions before moving to belief. We can see how this might go. Suppose two subjects have the same strange experience, perhaps that associated with the Capgras delusion. One subject forms the belief that *she is ill*, or perhaps she withholds judgement. The other subject *jumps to the conclusion* that *their loved one has been replaced by an imposter*. The presence of this bias has been claimed to gain support from the now infamous Beads Task (see Garety et al. 1991: 196, Dudley et al. 1997: 252–6). In this task subjects are presented with two opaque jars of beads containing two colours in opposing ratios (e.g. 80:20 and 20:80). They are asked to say when they're confident that they know which jar beads are being drawn from. Subjects with delusions are found to request fewer beads before deciding on the jar, hence the charge of *jumping to conclusions*. The special irrationality displayed by subjects with delusions relates to basing conclusions on too little evidence.

However, it has been noted by advocates of the jumping to conclusions bias that, at least with respect to Bayesianism, the reasoning style displayed by subjects with delusions is not a failure of rationality.[37] Instead, subjects without delusions exhibit too much caution (Garety et al. 1991: 200). It is also questionable whether this bias does in fact characterise the belief formation of subjects with delusions. Justin Sulik and colleagues have shown that when 'careless participants' are removed from the data, the relationship between holding delusion-like beliefs and jumping to conclusions is 'severely attenuated' or 'disappeared entirely'. That's because careless participants are coded as being high in delusion-like beliefs in comparison with diligent participants, and careless participants request to see fewer beads (Sulik et al. 2023: 757, see also Ross et al. 2016). What might have looked like a relationship between delusion and bias might in fact have been the result of 'careless responding in a subset of research participants' (Sulik et al. 2023: 749).

Another suggestion is the *bias towards observational adequacy*, where subjects privilege observational data (that given in experience) over minimising adjustments to one's beliefs (Stone and Young 1997: 349–50). In the case of Capgras, the idea is that the anomalous experience when looking at one's loved one is given epistemic influence that outweighs the influence of one's background beliefs. The fact that Glen's daughter seems different to him figures much more powerfully in his belief formation than any background beliefs he

[37] Although this is a common claim, Ryan McKay (2015) has argued that there is 'no basis' for it, because, 'in the absence of relevant costs', the Bayesian algorithm (which tells us about the probabilities of events) cannot tell us anything about when it is rational to stop drawing beads (465, fn. 9).

might have about the likelihood of imposters. Subjects with delusions are abnormally irrational insofar as they improperly weight certain kinds of evidence.[38]

One issue with this suggestion is incomplete coverage – in some cases of delusion (e.g. anosognosia, where a subject denies having some impairment), 'there is observational data crying out to be explained' in favour of the non-delusional belief, and so the subject should not be described as privileging what is observed (Noordhof and Sullivan-Bissett 2021: 10277–309). In addition, Davies and Coltheart have pointed out that if subjects had a bias of this kind, they should be more easily taken in by visual illusions. There is though no evidence for this (Davies and Coltheart 2000: 25–7).

Another way of being a two-factor theorist is to appeal to a *deficit* rather than a bias. Davies and colleagues locate the second factor not in belief formation, but in belief *evaluation*. According to this view, what needs explaining isn't why the subject forms the delusional belief, but rather why they keep hold of it, in the face of counterevidence. Davies and colleagues (2001) understand the second factor as 'the loss of the ability to reject a candidate for belief on the grounds of its implausibility and its inconsistency with everything else that the patient knows' (154).

However, subjects with delusions are often able to evaluate their beliefs for plausibility (even if they cannot bring themselves to abandon them), which suggests that they are perfectly well able to process information regarding a belief's plausibility. For example, a Capgras subject, when asked what he would think were someone to tell his story, replied 'I would find it extremely hard to believe' (Alexander et al. 1979: 335). This case has been taken to suggest that at least some people with delusions display 'considerable *appreciation of the implausibility* of their delusional beliefs' (Davies et al. 2001: 149, see also Gerrans 2001: 171). If that's right, there is no deficit with the processing of information regarding the plausibility of a belief, it is only that that information is not acted upon. If that's the source of the abnormal irrationality in delusion, then we are back to considering how people with delusions relate to evidence.

The final way of being a two-factor theorist is to be a *performance error* theorist. Gerrans (2001) distinguishes procedural from pragmatic irrationality,

[38] Kengo Miyazono and Alessandro Salice (2021) have offered an account of why subjects with delusions weight evidence from observation over the testimony of folk speaking to the implausibility of the delusion. They posit *testimonial abnormalities*, in particular: *testimonial isolation* (a lack of testimonial interactions with others), and *testimonial discount* (an arbitrarily selective neglect of testimony from others). McKay and Hugo Mercier (2023) have put forward a similar account, on which subjects with delusions are epistemically hypervigilant to the testimony of others.

identifying the problem with delusional belief formation in the latter. Pragmatic rationality is understood as the faculty employed to answer questions like 'What counts as good evidence? . . . How are initial probabilities assigned?' (162). On this view, subjects with delusions have the competence to, for example, form or evaluate beliefs appropriately, but they fail to put that competence into practice. Gerrans (2001) doesn't say much about what causes the performance failure (his interest in establishing a failure of *performance* rather than *competence*), but suggests that the issue is 'possibly based in the cause of [the] anomalous experience' (170). Of course, appeals to performance errors are open to one- and two-factor theorists alike, what will then need determining is whether the error in performance is one that could be explained as normally irrational, or not.

4.5.2 Summary Remarks

We noted that although there is logical space for the view that delusions are *rational* responses to anomalous experience, the argumentative action really lies in whether the irrationality of delusion is best understood as everyday or abnormal. Several features of delusion might support the latter judgement: their inconsistency or poor coherence with one's background beliefs, their poor relationship with evidence, and their highly implausible contents suggestive of severely impaired capacities for hypothesis selection. Two-factor theories might well take these features as friendly to their view; indeed several candidate second factors have been posited to explain an irrationality exhibited in cases of delusion which looks to go beyond what we see in normal cognition. We saw though that the one-factor approach, according to which the irrationality of delusion is everyday, had things to say about these features, such that they need not be understood as evidence in favour of abnormal irrationality.

4.6 Concluding Remarks

In general (notwithstanding noted exceptions), it is pretty uncontroversial that the beliefs we have discussed in this section are irrational. Why so? Because they all violate several plausible rationality constraints on belief. The debates concern how such irrationality arises. We have seen a range of possibilities – from cognitive biases which influence the processing of data, to motivational biases which might prompt one to prefer a belief with a certain feature. In the case of delusion – often taken to exhibit irrationality of an extreme kind – we saw that our usual resources for explaining the generation or maintenance of an irrational belief are often taken to be inadequate, and that a more severe, abnormal kind of irrationality must be posited. For my money, that's a mistake, and delusions can perfectly well take their place alongside other strange beliefs. Where appearances suggest they involve more serious errors of reasoning, we can pay attention to the context in which they arrive and thrive (that of anomalous experience). More generally, the everyday irrationalities to which we are all prone can go a long way to help us understand strange beliefs of many stripes, even when at first blush they strike us as incomprehensible or, at least, to have arisen from such poor epistemic performance as to seem resistant to ordinary theorising.

5 Implicit Bias

We turn now to our final case: implicit bias. We'll follow Jules Holroyd in understanding implicit biases as 'the processes or states that have a distorting influence on behaviour and judgment, and are detected in experimental conditions with implicit measures' (Holroyd 2016: 154). Implicit biases are posited as mental items which influence common microbehaviours or discriminations which cannot be tracked, predicted, or explained by a subject's explicit attitudes.

We'll begin with some examples. Sue interprets neutral behaviour as *aggressive* in Malcolm (who is a Black man), whilst that same behaviour performed by a White man would not strike her as such. Tracey walks into a job interview and presumes that the company Director 'Alex' (with whom she's corresponded over email) is the man at the table, and not any of the three women (a dynamic inverted for comic effect in the boardroom scene of Greta Gerwig's *Barbie*, 2023). Conor anxiously takes stock of his surroundings when Ahmed (a Muslim man) boards the tube carriage he was previously perfectly content traveling on. Let us suppose that Sue, Tracey, and Conor have beliefs concerning Black men, company directors, and Muslims respectively which would not explain their behaviour. We can even suppose that their beliefs are precisely the opposite of what we might expect given their behaviour.[39] Sue is active in the Black Lives Matter movement with a particular interest in policing; Tracey is a company director herself who spends a lot of time mentoring talented junior women; and Conor is a political scientist with a research interest in how best to address islamophobia in the UK. Any explicit attitudes our subjects would claim to have would not explain their behaviour.

[39] Such cases exemplify what Holroyd has called *conflict cases*, where the implicit bias a subject has *conflicts with* her explicit beliefs or values (Holroyd 2016: 158). Holroyd argues that other kinds of case are also important for our theorising, naming those where an individual's implicit bias aligns with their explicit beliefs and values, and those where this is so, but the subject is motivated to behave in line with egalitarian procedures. I focus on conflict cases because these are the most striking when we're thinking about rationality.

It is here that implicit biases enter the explanatory picture. Sue interprets Malcolm's behaviour as aggressive *because* she has an implicit bias against Black men; Tracey presumes that the man at the table is the company Director *because* she has an implicit bias against women; Conor becomes anxious when Ahmed boards the tube carriage *because* he has an implicit bias against Muslims. The vagueness with which I've specified the implicit biases in our examples – as well as my silence on exactly how they are explanatory of behaviour – is an artefact of the difficulty in approximating precision without first adopting a theory about the nature of implicit bias. And without such a theory, it's very difficult to say anything about irrationality either. We are thus situated a bit differently in comparison with the other cases of irrationality we have discussed up to this point. Let us see why.

In previous sections we have thought about akrasia, which, if it exhibits irrationality at all, exhibits the practical kind. And we have looked at a range of strange beliefs whose irrationality, where it is present, is of the epistemic kind. We learned that our judgements regarding the rationality of an attitude depend in part on the nature of that attitude, and we proceeded with a background of doxasticism for all our cases. Implicit bias is trickier. There are several ways to approach understanding what we refer to when we talk of *implicit bias*, and the various approaches will determine the range of what we can say about implicit bias and rationality.

Let's start easy. Sometimes the term *implicit bias* is used to refer to *biased behaviour* caused by an implicit attitude (e.g. Mandelbaum 2016: 631), but more often the term is used to refer to a *mental item* (to use a deliberately imprecise term) which causes biased behaviour. I'll opt for the latter usage. This is, of course, merely terminological – both uses of the term allow us to distinguish between certain behaviours and mental items responsible for them, and it is the latter that is usually taken to be the phenomenon of interest, insofar as it *explains* the former.

Other differences in the use of the term *implicit bias* cannot be put aside as mere artefacts of terminological preference. Let us begin with two streams of research in the field of implicit social cognition, labelled by Michael Brownstein (2018) as *True Attitudes* and *Driven Underground* (266; see also Payne and Gawronski 2010). The first arose from cognitive theories of learning and selective attention, and identifies two ways that information is processed: *automatic* and *controlled*. According to this approach, we do not have two different attitudes within a subject towards the same object, but rather two kinds of information processing, and there are two kinds of measurement instruments (direct and indirect), where the *indirect* measurement is thought to get us to a subject's *true attitude*.

Russ Fazio's (1990) *Motivation and Opportunity as Determinants (MODE) model* falls into the *True Attitude* approach. The idea is that when subjects are motivated to deliberate, and have the opportunity to do so, they are able to respond to direct measures of attitude which allow for time and cognitive resources, and are based on self-report. But indirect measures give us access to automatically processed information when control is taken away, and this information is representative of one's *true* attitude. On this model, Sue, Tracey, and Conor are misreporting their egalitarian attitudes, and, in fact, the only attitudes they have towards Black men, women, and Muslims, are the biased ones explanatory of their behaviour.

Alternatively, the *Driven Underground* stream allows for dissociated attitudes towards the same target object. Theories in this stream allow for implicit and explicit processes and mental constructs, and give *awareness* a key role in distinguishing the implicit from the explicit. Those theories which endorse the implicit-explicit cognition distinction posit distinct implicit and explicit processes. These are said to be characteristic of implicit and explicit mental constructs: one automatic, one controlled. On this approach, Sue, Tracey, and Conor have *two* kinds of attitude towards particular social groups: their explicit or avowed egalitarian attitudes, and their implicit attitudes explanatory of their biased behaviour. In what follows I'll focus on this second stream, following the trend in recent philosophical work.

Several kinds of *indirect measures* have been used to identify implicit bias; the most common is the Implicit Association Test (IAT).[40] IATs measure the speed at which subjects are able to pair two categories of objects (e.g. pictures of *old* and *young* faces) with, for example, pleasant and unpleasant stimuli (e.g. the words *wonderful* and *horrible*). The idea is that the speed and accuracy in the categorisation performance of combinations of categories can give us insight into which categories a subject *associates* with another (De Houwer et al. 2009:

[40] You can take versions of this test here: https://implicit.harvard.edu/implicit/takeatest.html. A pinch of salt should be administered with results for two reasons. First, implicit biases aren't static. You could complete an IAT on race, and get a different result in different conditions (i.e. under cognitive load, hunger, fatigue, etc.) Second, implicit biases concerning the same social groups do not travel together. A subject may score a certain way on an IAT testing for associations between a social group and negative valence (perhaps low bias), but score differently on an IAT testing for associations between that same social group and a stereotypical trait (perhaps high bias) (Amodio and Devine 2006). One way of explaining this experimental outcome is to understand the IAT as tracking two kinds of association (semantic and affective) (see Holroyd and Sweetman 2016: 92ff). There has also been recent discussion on how useful the IAT (among other indirect measures) is for predicting prejudiced behaviour (see e.g. Oswald et al. 2013 and Brownstein et al. 2020 for discussion).

347). (For an overview of other indirect measures see Sullivan-Bissett 2023: sect. 2; for more on what exactly such measures are measuring see Brownstein, Madva, and Gawronski 2019.)

5.1 Associationism

The standard view in philosophy and psychology is that implicit biases are *associations*. We all have stored associations, many in common with one another, some more unique to our personal circumstances. For most folk, when someone says *salt*, they think *pepper*. For many folk, when someone says *Laurel*, they think *Hardy*. For me, when someone says *labour*, I think of the British Labour Party and their electoral chances, whilst a midwife or a woman who had recently given birth may be put in mind of something very different. These examples demonstrate the genesis of associations as residing in the learning history of the subject (Levy 2015: 803). To say that implicit biases are associations is to say something like this: Conor's bias consists in a stored association between a particular concept (i.e. *Muslim male*) and a particular (negative) valence. In the presence of certain stimuli (e.g. seeing a Muslim male enter the train carriage), that stored association is *activated*. Some theorists have also explicitly allowed for associations between concepts (Mandelbaum 2016: 630) (e.g. one's concept of *Black male* and one's concept of *aggression*, as we might ascribe to Sue).

5.1.1 Associationism and (Ir)rationality

If associationism is along the right lines, what does that tell us about the rationality or otherwise of implicit biases? A first thought might be that associations are arational – they're simply concepts and valences knocking up against each other in cognitive space, with their etiology and maintenance 'sensitive merely to experienced relations of spatiotemporal contiguity' (Madva 2016: 2662). On the other hand, many authors have suggested that some associations (like Tracey's in our example earlier) may well be *rational*, insofar as they're picking up on genuine correlations in the environment – it is rational for me to think of *pepper* when I hear *salt*, since they so often appear together. Daniel Kelly and Erica Roedder give the example of a common implicit bias associating men with science:

> Women, as a matter of fact, are not as well-represented in the sciences. [. . .] With respect to the issue of rationality, our point is that if implicit attitudes are construed in this very minimal way – as indicating only that a person associates two concepts – it appears they can be rational in some sense (e.g., insofar as the association between concepts accurately represents a correlation of

> statistical regularity that holds among those referents of the concepts). (Kelly and Roedder 2008: 529)[41]

This point concerning implicit associations tracking social realities has been developed most robustly by Tamar Gendler, who argues for the 'sad conclusion' that we must choose between explicit or implicit irrationality. Gendler focuses on the differential crime rates of White and Black people in America, noting that the base rate information (which shows that Black people are much more likely to commit homicide than White people),[42] should

> lead a person to update her prior probability; rationally, she should come to believe with respect to certain racial groups that the likelihood of a member of that racial group committing a certain sort of crime is higher than for a member of some other racial group. (Gendler 2011: 56)

On the other hand, a committed egalitarian may take some information to be suggestive of what Philip Tetlock and colleagues have called a *forbidden base rate*, too offensive to enter into one's probability calculations (Tetlock et al. 2000: 854). On the explicit side then, someone who rejects particular stereotypes or associations regarding members of certain groups neglects the base rate, and '[f]ailure to take into consideration background information about the relative distribution of properties is a classic failure of reasoning' (Gendler 2011: 34). On the other hand, for egalitarians at least, encoding associations concerning members of particular groups – associations which one reflectively rejects – is an instance of implicit irrationality. We could, of course, say that, as uncomfortable as the data is, if the egalitarian wants to exhibit good reasoning, the data cannot be ignored. But, as we have already noted, our egalitarian does not have an easy route to rationality. Even if she encodes the base rate data in her implicit associations, she now encodes associations that she reflectively rejects. Implicit biases then may not be irrational insofar as they encode real associations, but at least in some cases, their irrationality arises from their being in conflict with explicit attitudes of the subject.[43]

---

41 Kelly and Roedder go on to express scepticism about implicit bias being rational, noting that they suspect implicit associations 'almost always extend beyond what is rational, and there will almost always be a "remainder": an implicit association that goes beyond what rationality endorses' (2008: 530). At the very least, many implicit biases cannot be construed as tracking statistical realities (e.g. Conor's bias against Muslim males).

42 Gendler is rightly at great pains to point out that 'the explanation for these differences lies in the nation's legacy of racial injustice' (2011: 56).

43 Of course, perhaps the way of reconciling all of this is for the egalitarian to bring her explicit attitudes in line with the social realities, to not only encode base rate information in her implicit associations, but to positively endorse the truth of them. Any dissonance this causes might be soothed by reminding her that although members of group *x* are more likely to *y*, this can be explained in a way that doesn't involve endorsing any bigoted views about intrinsic properties of

Katherine Puddifoot understands Gendler as presenting an *ethical/epistemic* dilemma, requiring that we choose between epistemic demands that our beliefs reflect base rates, and ethical demands requiring that we treat people equally (Puddifoot 2017; 2021, Ch. 5). Puddifoot argues that although sometimes epistemic and ethical demands conflict, at other times, the goals of both are served by stereotyping, at other times, the goals of both are served by not stereotyping. Our predicament is thus more complicated, tasking us with identifying 'whether [we] are in a situation in which either or both of [our] epistemic or ethical goals can be achieved by stereotyping' (2021: 95). Rima Basu (2020) goes further, arguing that in cases where it might seem our epistemic and ethical goals are in conflict, what we in fact have is moral encroachment on the epistemic, where epistemic standards are raised by moral considerations.

Let us turn now to an alternative way to model implicit bias, and what that enables us to say about the rationality or otherwise of implicit bias.

5.2 Propositionalism

Although I identified associationism as the *standard view*, recently some authors have made the case for a radically different way of modelling implicit biases: propositionalism. States with propositional contents have satisfaction conditions, whereas states with only associative contents do not; instead, associative contents are '(relations among) mental representations that lack any syntactic structure' (Mandelbaum 2013: 199, fn. 1).

The case for propositionalism has been made by appeal to empirical work demonstrating that implicit biases are vulnerable to what Gabbrielle Johnson (2020) calls *rational intervention*, understood as 'an attempt to intervene on a person's implicit attitudes that relies on the informational content of the intervention (the reasons they present) rather than mere repeated exposure to the intervention' (28–9). The case for propositionalism on these grounds has been most robustly made by Eric Mandelbaum (2016). He overviews empirical work that shows that implicit biases are modulated by logical and evidential considerations (see Toribio 2018: 41). In particular, they follow the logic of 'the enemy of my enemy is my friend' (Gawronski et al. 2005), they are sensitive to argument strength (Briñol et al. 2009), and they are adjustable in light of peer judgement (Sechrist and Stangor 2001).

Of course, even if we find the case for propositionalism compelling, that doesn't settle the question of what exactly implicit biases are. All sorts of mental states have propositional contents. Take the proposition *implicit biases are*

members of group *x*. Perhaps this is what rationality requires. I suspect that, faced with this, egalitarians may be inclined to the view that rationality is not worth the cost.

difficult to theorise about. That could be the content of a belief, an imagining, a supposing, or even a (strange) desire. Propositionalism thus narrows the attitudinal possibilities, but there are still discoveries to be made.

Mandelbaum's view is that implicit biases are *unconscious beliefs*. Sue's implicit bias is best understood as the unconscious belief that *Black men are aggressive*, Tracey's as the unconscious belief that *women are not leaders*, and Conor's as the unconscious belief that *Muslims are dangerous*. Mandelbaum argues that this view can accommodate the empirical results supporting propositionalism.

A couple of other models which cast implicit biases as propositional are worth mentioning here. One comes from Levy (2015), according to which implicit biases are *patchy endorsements*. The *endorsement* part is that a subject commits to the world being as the proposition picks out, and the *patchy* part is in recognition of the fact that biases respond to only some sorts of evidence and feature in only some sorts of inference. On another, hybrid, view implicit biases are *constituted by* unconscious imaginings, at least some of which have propositional contents (Sullivan-Bissett 2019).[44] Let us turn to what we can say about the (ir)rationality of implicit biases when they are understood as propositional.

5.2.1 Propositionalism and (Ir)rationality

If implicit biases are beliefs, perhaps we can assess their rationality in much the same way as we did our phenomena in Section 4 – by appeal to rationality constraints on belief. First, consistency. In conflict cases like Sue's, Conor's, and Tracey's, our subjects have *inconsistent beliefs*: the egalitarian beliefs they are disposed to espouse, and their unconscious beliefs responsible for their biased behaviours. Second, an appropriate relationship to evidence. We have seen already in our discussion of base rates that things are complicated here, but we can certainly imagine cases where – even being properly responsive to base rates and other sources of evidence (a stereotype-endorsing media perhaps) – one's implicit bias goes beyond what that would suggest (see fn. 41).[45] At the very least,

[44] Other models that I won't discuss have it that implicit biases are *character traits* (Machery 2016), *aliefs* (Gendler 2011), or *mental imagery* (Nanay 2021).

[45] The rationality constraint of inferential coherence is tricky. If Conor believes that *almost all Muslims are ordinary folk* (and not dangerous conspirers against the West), then he should also believe that *that particular Muslim* (who boarded the subway carriage) *is almost certainly an ordinary guy* (and not a dangerous conspirer against the West). He probably would sincerely claim to believe this. So far, so coherent. If his unconscious belief is something like *Muslims are dangerous* he should also (unconsciously) believe that *that particular Muslim* (who boarded the subway carriage) *is dangerous*. It will depend on the particular details of a doxastic account whether this more specific content finds a home in Conor's implicit bias, but at the very least we

even if we think that implicit biases are accurately tracking base rates, many biases go further. Tracey's suite of biases against women might include one with the content *women are not leaders*, something which finds some support in base rates (for example, at the time of writing (June 2024), in the UK, only ten FTSE 100 company CEOs are women). Other biases of Tracey's though may cast women as bossy, or incompetent. And so, if one of the women in the boardroom introduces herself as Alex the company Director, we can forgive Tracey's mild surprise (after all, a woman director is relatively unusual), but we can't forgive her other behavioural responses to this fact (misinterpreting Alex as *officious* rather than *assertive*, taking Alex to be *slow* rather than *deliberative*, and so on). And biases of this kind may be resistant to revision in the face of counterevidence. It would not be science fiction to imagine that Alex could be the most inspiring and competent CEO in the land, and yet, due to the operation of implicit bias against women, she is not afforded the credibility she is due.

We have seen what we might say about implicit biases understood as beliefs, and might take our job in this section to be mostly done. However, things aren't so simple. Although Mandelbaum has become widely known as a proponent of a doxastic approach to bias, there's a sense in which this is a bit misleading. Key to Mandelbaum's overall position is his adoption of a Spinozan account of belief, according to which we *believe any truth-apt proposition that we represent*. According to this account, there is no gap between representing a truth-apt proposition and believing it, 'the act of understanding is the act of believing' (Gilbert et al. 1993: 222). The adoption of the Spinozan model of belief goes a long way to bridging the gap between the conclusion that biases are *propositional* and the conclusion that they are *beliefs* (of a Spinozan sort). Beliefs are very easy to come by once propositions are on the table. But of course, this is a fairly unorthodox way of thinking about the nature of belief, and in recognition of this Mandelbaum (2016) notes that if the term *belief* offends, readers should feel free to understand his hypothesis as one about *structured thoughts* (636). He is motivated primarily by the idea that implicit biases are propositional and not associative, rather than by identifying a particular attitudinal vehicle in which they reside.[46]

can see how the applicability of the rationality constraint of inferential coherence is not straightforward.

[46] And in case readers take this to be a quirk of Mandelbaum's philosophical motivations, it is not. Indeed, Frankish (2016), in referring readers looking for 'other belief-based accounts of implicit attitudes' (29, fn. 8), cites work which is concerned with structure, not attitudinal vehicle. In addition to Mandelbaum (2016), he refers to De Houwer (2014), in which it is argued that 'implicit evaluation is mediated by the formation or activation of propositions' (350); Sean Hughes and colleagues (2011) who, in a paper without a single token of the word 'belief', conclude that 'it seems reasonable to explore non-associative accounts of implicit attitudes' (488); and Chris J. Mitchell and colleagues (2009) who do indeed conclude that the

So what of the Spinozan view then? If implicit biases are Spinozan beliefs, can what we said earlier about their rationality be applied? It cannot. Once in the domain of Spinozan belief, the rationality constraints on belief that we've been working with have far less applicability. That's because Spinozan belief fixation is *arational*.[47] An instructive parallel is offered by Levy and Mandelbaum when they imagine that a subject, having been hit in the head with a brick, is caused to believe that *the universe has ten planets*. For Levy and Mandelbaum (2014), although this belief isn't *justified*, it isn't *irrational* either, and that's because 'it isn't bad reasoning that led you to this belief', rather, the belief was formed 'in a merely brute causal way' (22). And so it is with implicit biases understood as Spinozan beliefs. It is inappropriate to subject them to analysis regarding their being rational or irrational, because for something to be in the remit of such analysis, it has to be formed in a certain way, at the very least, not in a brutely causal way (22).

Of course, we might return to the idea of base rates and note that, at least in some cases, propositionally structured implicit biases are approximating to those, and so are *rational*. When Tracey forms the unconscious belief *women are not leaders* which is constitutive of her bias against women, we might construe her as picking up on genuine statistical correlations. There are two issues with this. The first is that propositionally structured implicit biases have been understood as taking a form more imprecise than social realities (Mandelbaum's (2016) own example is 'Black males are dangerous' (635)). This is a universally quantified statement which is categorically false, and sufficiently far from what base rates might suggest about Black males and danger. Associations on the other hand might be interpreted as less committal. Second, even if the propositional contents of implicit biases were sufficiently precise to approximate social realities, we still wouldn't have arrived at rationality. Something's being apt for rationality assessment goes beyond its contents, and depends on the way in which it is generated. Whilst it is natural enough to say that it is rational to *associate* x with *y* if such association is reflected in social realities, having a belief that reflects that association can still be irrational if its formation was brutely causal.[48]

'propositional approach suggests that these phenomena should be reinterpreted to be the consequence of propositional reasoning *leading to the acquisition of new beliefs*' (198, my emphasis), but under the umbrella of 'these phenomena' we do not find implicit bias, but rather a broader approach to associative learning.

[47] Federico Bongiorno (2022) has argued that Spinozan belief fixation gives us a new line of defence for doxasticism about delusions since those features appealed to in the service of non-doxasticism do not speak against belief understood in the Spinozan framework.

[48] Even other propositionalist models (Levy 2015; Sullivan-Bissett 2019) are not going to help us get closer to a judgement of irrationality for implicit bias, insofar as they too will be committed to the formation of propositionally structured implicit biases bypassing rational processes.

5.3 Concluding Remarks

We began this section by characterising implicit biases as mental items that influence behaviours and discriminations which were not explainable by appeal to a subject's explicit attitudes. From here the options open to us with respect to assessments of (ir)rationality depended on what we took implicit biases to be. According to the standard view, implicit biases are associations, and we saw a case for their being rational (insofar as they pick up on social realities). However, taken more broadly as items in an (egalitarian) subject's overall cognitive economy, we saw that living in a society with inequalities leaves us only options of irrationality. Don't encode the prejudiced biases which reflect social realities, or do encode them against one's reflective judgement.

On the other hand, propositionalists take implicit biases to have propositional contents, and indeed, the most thoroughgoing defence of propositionalism took them to be unconscious *beliefs*. We saw that the background account of belief in play here made it illegitimate to refer to our earlier rationality constraints on belief, given that belief formation on this account is brute. We considered whether implicit biases might be rationalised on this model by appeal to their reflecting social realities, but saw that this was problematic.

Overall, implicit biases are perhaps the most obvious occupants of our minds which demonstrate that the rational isn't always the good or the desired. Whereas it is natural to think that one should aim at rational action and rational belief formation, when it comes to implicit cognition shaped by social realities, things are considerably less clear.

6 Conclusion

Philosophical work on irrationality has benefited in the last few decades from empirical work in psychology, which has put some helpful empirical flesh on the otherwise more speculative bones. Bringing together philosophical and psychological work has helped researchers have a better understanding of the processes that contribute to a range of mental phenomena which strike us as irrational.

Over the course of this Element, we have thought about various cases typically taken to display irrationality. We understood irrationality as a departure from the proper application of rules of logic and probability, as well as various other principles of rational belief and action. We have seen that, even with this as our background, determining whether something is irrational is often not as easy as we might have expected. *Acting against one's better judgement is clearly irrational! You should do what you think it is best to do!* But what if our account of practical rationality should be more holistic? What if we should take rationality to consist in more than being guided in action by one's better judgement alone? *Believing that COVID-19 is a side effect of 5G towers is clearly irrational! You should form beliefs in line with the evidence!* But what if conspiracy theorists *are* forming their beliefs in line with the evidence? Might they be rational believers in an epistemically polluted environment? *Having an implicit bias against women in science is clearly irrational! Women are equally able scientists, and being biased against them is getting something wrong about the world, as well as being complicit in perpetuating injustice!* But what if attending to base rates is a requirement of rationality? What if our implicit biases are appropriately tracking social realities?

Even when we agree that we have a case of irrationality, there are still discoveries to be made about why that is so, and whether that irrationality goes beyond the everyday. We might all agree that beliefs issuing from self-deception are irrational. But why? Because they result from an intention to form a false belief? Because they are inconsistent with our other beliefs? Because they are the consequence of the operation of cognitive biases? And we might all agree that delusional beliefs are irrational. But given how bizarre and entrenched these beliefs can be, do we need to posit a more extreme form of irrationality to understand what's going on? Characterising something as irrational is, thus, only a starting point. Making good on that characterisation is where the interesting philosophical action is.

Overall, I hope this Element has, by looking through the lens of (ir)rationality, given the reader a better understanding of the various psychological phenomena we have surveyed. I also (perhaps more ambitiously) hope that the reader arrives at this point with sympathy for the following thought: some of the more disparaged aspects of our mental lives should not simply be condemned to the rubbish bin of irrationality, with our implicit aim understood as *less of that stuff please!* Things are, as we have seen, considerably more complicated than such an approach could possibly recognise. Our mental lives are thorny, fascinating, and rich, and our understanding of them should appreciate them in their entirety, irrational warts and all.

References

American Psychiatric Association 2013: *Diagnostic and Statistical Manual of Mental Disorders*: DSM-5. Washington, DC: American Psychiatric Association.

Ames, David 1984: 'Self-Shooting of a Phantom Head'. *The British Journal of Psychiatry*. Vol. 145, no. 2, pp. 193–4.

Amodio, David M. and Devine, Patricia G. 2006: 'Stereotyping and Evaluation in Implicit Race Bias: Evidence for Independent Constructs and Unique Effects on Behavior'. *Journal of Personality and Social Psychology*, Vol. 91, pp. 652–61.

Archer, Sophie 2013: 'Nondoxasticism about Self-Deception'. *Dialectica*. Vol. 67, no. 3, pp. 265–82.

Arpaly, Nomy 2000: 'On Acting Rationally against One's Best Judgment'. *Ethics*. Vol. 110, no. 3, pp. 488–513.

Audi, Robert 1982: 'Self-Deception, Action and Will'. *Erkenntnis*. Vol. 18, no. 2, pp. 133–58.

Audi, Robert 1990: 'Weakness of Will and Rational Action'. *Australasian Journal of Philosophy*. Vol. 68, no. 2, pp. 270–81.

Basu, Rima 2020: 'The Specter of Normative Conflict: Does Fairness Require Inaccuracy?' In Beeghly, Erin and Madva, Alex (eds.) *An Introduction to Implicit Bias: Knowledge, Justice, and the Social Mind*. New York: Routledge, pp. 191–210.

Bayne, Tim and Pacherie, Elisabeth 2004: 'Bottom-Up or Top-Down: Campbell's Rationality Account of Monothematic Delusions'. *Philosophy, Psychiatry, & Psychology*. Vol. 11, pp. 1–11.

Begby, Endre 2021: 'Evidential Preemption'. *Philosophy and Phenomenological Research*. Vol. 102, pp. 515–30.

Bentall, Richard P., Corcoran, Rhiannon, Howard, Robert, Blackwood, Nigel, and Kinderman, Peter 2001: 'Persecutory Delusions: A Review and Theoretical Integration'. *Clinical Psychology Review*. Vol. 21, no. 8, pp. 1143–92.

Bermúdez, José Luis 2000: 'Self-Deception, Intentions, and Contradictory Beliefs'. *Analysis*. Vol. 60, no. 4, pp. 309–19.

Bermúdez, José Luis 2001: 'Normativity and Rationality in Delusional Psychiatric Disorders'. *Mind & Language*. Vol. 16, no. 5, pp. 457–93.

Berrios, Germán E. 1991: 'Delusions as "Wrong Beliefs": A Conceptual History'. *British Journal of Psychiatry*. Vol. 159, pp. 6–13.

Bongiorno, Federico 2022: 'Spinozan Doxasticism about Delusions'. *Pacific Philosophical Quarterly*. Vol. 103, no. 4, pp. 720–52.

Bortolotti, Lisa 2009: *Delusions and Other Irrational Beliefs*. New York: Oxford University Press.

Bortolotti, Lisa 2015a: *Irrationality*. Cambridge: Polity.

Bortolotti, Lisa 2015b: 'The Epistemic Innocence of Motivated Delusions'. *Consciousness and Cognition*. Vol. 33, pp. 490–99.

Bortolotti, Lisa 2016: 'Epistemic Benefits of Elaborated and Systematized Delusions in Schizophrenia'. *British Journal for the Philosophy of Science*. Vol. 67, no. 3, pp. 879–900.

Bortolotti, Lisa 2018: 'Stranger than Fiction: Costs and Benefits of Everyday Confabulation'. *Review of Philosophy and Psychology*. Vol. 9, pp. 227–49.

Bortolotti, Lisa 2020: *The Epistemic Innocence of Irrational Beliefs*. Oxford: Oxford University Press.

Bortolotti, Lisa and Broome, Matthew 2008: 'Delusional Beliefs and Reason Giving'. *Philosophical Psychology*. Vol. 21, no. 6, pp. 821–41.

Bortolotti, Lisa and Sullivan-Bissett, Ema 2020: 'The Epistemic Innocence of Clinical Memory Distortions'. *Mind & Language*. Vol. 3, no. 3, pp. 263–79.

Bratman, Michael 1979: 'Practical Reasoning and Weakness of the Will'. *Noûs*. Vol. 13, no. 2, pp. 153–71.

Briñol, Pablo, Petty, Richard E., and McCaslin, Michael J. 2009: 'Changing Attitudes on Implicit Versus Explicit Measures: What Is the Difference?' In Petty, Richard E., Fazio, Russell H., and Briñol, Pablo (eds.) *Attitudes: Insights from the New Implicit Measures*. New York: Psychology Press, pp. 285–326.

Brotherton, Rob 2015: *Suspicious Minds: Why We Believe Conspiracy Theories*. London: Bloomsbury Sigma.

Brotherton, Rob, and French, Christopher. C. 2015: 'Intention Seekers: Conspiracist Ideation and Biased Attributions of Intentionality'. *PLoS ONE*. Vol. 10, no. 5, e0124125.

Brownstein, Michael 2018: 'Implicit Bias and Race'. In Taylor, Paul C., Alcoff, Linda Martin, and Anderson, Luvell (eds.) *The Routledge Companion to the Philosophy of Race*. New York: Routledge, pp. 261–76.

Brownstein, Michael, Madva, Alex, and Gawronski, Bertram 2019: 'What Do Implicit Measures Measure?' *WIREs Cognitive Science*. Vol. 10, no. 5, e1501.

Brownstein, Michael, Madva, Alex, and Gawronski, Bertram 2020: 'Understanding Implicit Bias: Putting the Criticism into Perspective'. *Pacific Philosophical Quarterly*. Vol. 101, no. 2, pp. 276–307.

Campbell, John 2001: 'Rationality, Meaning, and the Analysis of Delusion'. *Philosophy, Psychiatry & Psychology*. Vol. 8, pp. 89–100.

Carr, Jennifer Rose 2022: 'Why Ideal Epistemology?'. *Mind*. Vol. 131, pp. 1131–62.

Cassam, Quassim 2018: 'Epistemic Insouciance'. *Journal of Philosophical Research*. Vol. 43, pp. 1–20.

Coady, David 2003: 'Conspiracy Theories and Official Stories'. *International Journal of Applied Philosophy*. Vol. 17, no. 2, pp. 199–211.

Coltheart, Max and Davies, Martin 2021: 'Failure of Hypothesis Evaluation as a Factor in Delusional Belief'. *Cognitive Neuropsychiatry*. Vol. 26, no. 4, pp. 213–60.

Coltheart, Max, Langdon, Robyn , and McKay, Ryan 2007: 'Schizophrenia and Monothematic Delusions'. *Schizophrenia Bulletin*. Vol. 33, no. 3, pp. 642–7.

Coltheart, Max, Menzies, Peter, and Sutton, John 2010: 'Abductive Inference and Delusional Belief'. *Cognitive Neuropsychiatry*. Vol. 24, no. 3, pp. 165–77.

Coppock, Alexander 2022: *Persuasion in Parallel*. Chicago, IL: University of Chicago Press.

Corlett, Philip, Taylor, Jane R., Wang, Xiao-Jing, Fletcher, Paul C., and Krystal, John H. 2010: 'Toward a Neurobiology of Delusions'. *Progress in Neurobiology*. Vol. 92, pp. 345–69.

Crimmins, Mark 1992: 'I Falsely Believe That P'. *Analysis*. Vol. 52, no. 3, p. 191.

Currie, Gregory 2000: 'Imagination, Hallucination and Delusion'. *Mind & Language*. Vol. 15, pp. 168–83.

Davidson, Donald 1980: 'How Is Weakness of the Will Possible?' In Davidson, Donald (ed.) *Essays on Actions and Events: Philosophical Essays Volume 1*. Oxford: Oxford University Press, pp. 21–42.

Davidson, Donald 1982: 'Paradoxes of Irrationality'. In Wollheim, Richard, and Hopkins, James (eds.) *Philosophical Essays on Freud*. Cambridge: Cambridge University Press, pp. 289–305.

Davies, Martin and Coltheart, Max 2000: 'Introduction: Pathologies of Belief'. *Mind and Language*. Vol. 15, no. 1, pp. 1–46.

Davies, Martin, Coltheart, Max, Langdon, Robyn, and Breen, Nora 2001: 'Monothematic Delusions: Towards a Two-Factor Account'. *Philosophy, Psychiatry, & Psychology*. Vol. 8, nos. 2–3, pp. 133–58.

Davies, Martin, Davies, Aimola Anna, and Coltheart, Max 2005: 'Anosognosia and the Two-Factor Theory of Delusions'. *Mind and Language*. Vol. 20, no. 2, pp. 209–36.

Dawkins, Richard 2006: *The God Delusion*. London: Bantam Press.

De Houwer, Jan, Teige-Mocigemba, Sarah, Spruyt, Adriaan, and Moors, Agnes 2009: 'Implicit Measures: A Normative Analysis and Review'. *Psychological Bulletin*. Vol. 135, pp. 347–68.

De Houwer, Jan 2014: 'A Propositional Model of Implicit Evaluation'. *Social and Personality Psychology Compass*. Vol. 8, no. 7, pp. 342–53.

Dentith, Matthew R. X. 2018: 'The Problem of Conspiracism'. *Argumenta*. Vol. 3, no. 2, pp. 327–43.

DeRose, Keith 1992: 'Contextualism and Knowledge Attributions'. *Philosophy and Phenomenological Research*. Vol. 52, no. 4, pp. 913–29.

Dodd, Dylan 2009: 'Weakness of Will as Intention-Violation'. *European Journal of Philosophy*. Vol. 17, no. 1, pp. 45–59.

Douglas, Karen M. and Sutton, Robbie M. 2023: 'What Are Conspiracy Theories? A Definitional Approach to Their Correlates, Consequences, and Communication'. *Annual Review of Psychology*. Vol. 74, pp. 271–98.

Douglas, Karen M., Sutton, Robbie M., Callan, Mitch J., Dawtry, Rael J., and Harvey, Annelie J. 2016: 'Someone is Pulling the Strings: Hypersensitive Agency Detection and Belief in Conspiracy Theories'. *Thinking and Reasoning*. Vol. 22, no. 1, pp. 57–77.

Dub, Richard 2017: 'Delusions, Acceptances, and Cognitive Feelings'. *Philosophy and Phenomenological Research*. Vol. 94, no. 1, pp. 27–60.

Dudley, Robert E. J., John, Carolyn H., Young, Andrew W., and Over, David E. 1997: 'Normal and Abnormal Reasoning in People with Delusions'. *British Journal of Clinical Psychology*. Vol. 36, pp. 243–58.

Ebel-Lam, Anna, Fabrigar, Leandre R., MacDonald, Tara K., and Jones, Sarah 2010: 'Balancing Causes and Consequences: The Magnitude-Matching Principle in Explanations for Complex Social Events'. *Basic and Applied Social Psychology*. Vol. 32, no. 4, pp. 348–59.

Egan, Andy 2008: 'Imagination, Delusion, and Self-Deception'. In Bayne, Tim and Fernandez, Jordi (eds.) *Delusion and Self-Deception*. New York: Psychology Press, pp. 263–80.

Fazio, Russ 1990: 'Multiple Processes by Which Attitudes Guide Behavior: The MODE Model as an Integrative Framework'. *Advances in Experimental Social Psychology*. Vol. 23, pp. 75–109.

Frankish, Keith 2009: 'Delusions: A Two-level Framework'. In Broome, Matthew and Bortolotti, Lisa (eds.) *Psychiatry as Cognitive Neuroscience: Philosophical Perspectives*. Oxford: Oxford University Press, pp. 269–84.

Frankish, Keith 2016: 'Playing Double: Implicit Bias, Dual Levels, and Self-Control'. In Brownstein, Michael and Saul, Jennifer (eds.) *Implicit Bias and Philosophy, Vol. 1: Metaphysics and Epistemology*. Oxford: Oxford University Press, pp. 23–46.

Fine, Cordelia, Craigie, Frankieian, and Gold, Ian 2005: 'The Explanation Approach to Delusion'. *Philosophy, Psychiatry, and Psychology*. Vol. 12, no. 2, pp. 159–63.

Flores, Carolina *forthcoming*: 'Why Think that Belief Is Evidence-Responsive?' In Jong, Jonathan and Schwitzgebel, Eric (Eds.) *The Nature of Belief*. Oxford University Press.

Friedrich, James 1993: 'Primary Error Detection and Minimization (PEDMIN) Strategies in Social Cognition: A Reinterpretation of Confirmation Bias Phenomena'. *Psychological Review*. Vol. 100, pp. 298–319.

Funkhouser, Eric 2005: 'Do the Self-Deceived Get What They Want?' *Pacific Philosophical Quarterly*. Vol. 86, no. 3, pp. 295–312.

Gao, Jie 2020: 'Self-Deception and Pragmatic Encroachment: A Dilemma for Epistemic Rationality'. *Ratio*. Vol. 34, pp. 20–32.

Garety, Philippa A., Hemsley, David R., and Wessely, Simon 1991: 'Reasoning in Deluded Schizophrenic and Paranoid Patients: Biases in Performance on a Probabilistic Inference Task'. *The Journal of Nervous and Mental Disease*. Vol. 179, no. 4, pp. 194–201.

Gawronski, Bertram, Walther, Eva, and Blank, Hartmut 2005: 'Cognitive Consistency and the Formation of Interpersonal Attitudes: Cognitive Balance Affects the Encoding of Social Information'. *Journal of Experimental and Social Psychology*. Vol. 41, pp. 618–26.

Gendler, Tamar Szabó 2007: 'Self-Deception as Pretense'. *Philosophical Perspectives*. Vol. 21, pp. 231–58.

Gendler, Tamar 2011: 'On the Epistemic Costs of Implicit Bias'. *Philosophical Studies*. Vol. 156, pp. 33–63.

Gerrans, Philip 2000: 'Refining the Explanation of Cotard's Delusion'. *Mind & Language*. Vol. 15, no. 1, pp. 111–22.

Gerrans, Philip 2001: 'Delusions as Performance Failures'. *Cognitive Neuropsychiatry*. Vol. 6, no. 3, pp. 161–73.

Gerrans, Philip 2002: 'A One-stage Explanation of the Cotard Delusion'. *Philosophy, Psychiatry, and Psychology*. Vol. 9, no. 1, pp. 47–53.

Gerrans, Philip 2024: 'Cotard Syndrome: The Experience of Inexistence'. In Sullivan-Bissett, Ema (ed.) *Belief, Imagination, and Delusion*. Oxford: Oxford University Press, pp. 181–204.

Gibson, Quinn Hiroshi 2020: 'Self-Deception as Omission'. *Philosophical Psychology*. Vol. 33, no. 5, pp. 657–78.

Gilbert, Dan T., Tafarodi, Romin W., and Malone, Patrick S. 1993: 'You Can't Not Believe Everything You Read'. *Attitudes and Social Cognition*. Vol. 65, no. 2, pp. 221–33.

Gold, Ian and Gold, Joel 2024: 'Delusion and Culture'. In Sullivan-Bissett, Ema (ed.) *The Routledge Handbook of the Philosophy of Delusion*. Oxon: Routledge, pp. 533–543.

Griggs, Richard A. and Cox, James R. 1982: 'The Elusive Thematic-Materials Effect in Wason's Selection Task'. *British Journal of Psychology*. Vol. 73, pp. 407–20.

Helton, Grace 2018: 'If You Can't Change What You Believe, You Don't Believe It'. *Noûs*. Vol. 54, no. 3, pp. 501–26.

Hertwig, Ralph, Leuker, Christina, Pachur, Thorsten, Spiliopoulos, Leonidas, and Pleskac, Timothy J. 2022: 'Studies in Ecological Rationality'. *Topics in Cognitive Science*. Vol. 14, pp. 467–91.

Holroyd, Jules 2016: 'What Do We Want from a Model of Implicit Cognition?' *Proceedings of the Aristotelian Society*. Vol. CXVI, no. 2, pp. 153–79.

Holroyd, Jules and Sweetman, Joseph 2016: 'The Heterogeneity of Implicit Bias'. In Brownstein, Michael and Saul, Jennifer (eds.) *Implicit Bias and Philosophy. Volume one. Metaphysics and Epistemology*. Oxford: Oxford University Press: 80–103.

Holton, Richard 1999: 'Intention and Weakness of Will'. *The Journal of Philosophy*. Vol. 96, no. 5, pp. 241–62.

Holton, Richard 2009: *Willing, Wanting, Waiting*. Oxford: Clarendon Press.

Hubin, Donald C. 1990: 'Irrational Desires'. *Philosophical Studies*. Vol. 62, pp. 23–44.

Hughes, Sean, Barnes-Holmes, Dermot, and De Houwer, Jan 2011: 'The Dominance of Associative Theorizing in Implicit Attitude Research: Propositional and Behavioural Alternatives'. *The Psychological Record*. Vol. 61, pp. 465–96.

Hume, David 1739/2004: *A Treatise of Human Nature*. New York: Dover.

Ichino, Anna 2020: 'Superstitious Confabulations'. *Topoi*. Vol. 39, pp. 203–17.

Ichino, Anna 2024: 'Religious Imaginings'. In Sullivan-Bissett, Ema (ed.) *Belief, Imagination, and Delusion*. Oxford: Oxford University Press.

Ichino, Anna and Räikkä, Juha 2021: 'Non-Doxastic Conspiracy Theories'. *Argumenta*. Vol. 7, no.1, pp. 247–63.

Johnson, Gabbrielle 2020: 'The Psychology of Bias'. In Beeghly, Erin and Madva, Alex (eds.) *An Introduction to Implicit Bias: Knowledge, Justice, and the Social Mind*. Routledge, pp. 20–40.

Johnson-Laird, Phil N., Legrenzi, Paolo, and Sonino Legrenzi, Maria 1972: 'Reasoning and Sense of Reality'. *British Journal of Psychology*. Vol. 63, pp. 395–400.

Kiesewetter, Benjamin and Worsnip, Alex 2023: 'Structural Rationality'. In Zalta, Edward N. and Nodelman, Uri (eds.) *The Stanford Encyclopedia of Philosophy* (Fall 2023 Edition). URL: https://plato.stanford.edu/entries/rationality-structural/

Kelly, Daniel and Roedder, Erica 2008: 'Racial Cognition and the Ethics of Implicit Bias'. *Philosophy Compass*. Vol. 3, no. 3, pp. 522–40.

Kvanvig, Jonathan L. 2011: 'Against Pragmatic Encroachment'. *Logos & Episteme*. Vol. II, no. 1, pp. 77–85.

Lackey, Jennifer 2021: 'Echo Chambers, Fake News, and Social Epistemology'. In Bernecker, Sven, Flowerree, Amy K., and Grundmann, Thomas (eds.) *The Epistemology of Fake News*. Oxford: Oxford University Press, pp. 206–27.

Leary, Stephanie 2017: 'In Defense of Practical Reasons for Belief'. *Australasian Journal of Philosophy*. Vol. 95, no. 3, pp. 529–42.

Leitgeb, Hannes 2014: 'A Way Out of the Preface Paradox?' *Analysis*. Vol. 74, no. 1, pp. 11–15.

Leman, Patrick J. and Cinnirella, Marco 2007: 'A Major Event has a Major Cause: Evidence for the Role of Heuristics in Reasoning about Conspiracy Theories'. *Social Psychology Review*. Vol. 9, no. 2, pp. 18–28.

Letheby, Christopher 2015: 'The Epistemic Innocence of Psychedelic States'. *Consciousness and Cognition*. Vol. 39, pp. 28–37.

Levy, Neil 2015: 'Neither Fish Nor Fowl: Implicit Attitudes as Patchy Endorsements'. *Noûs*. Vol. 49, no. 4, pp. 800–23.

Levy, Neil 2021: *Bad Beliefs: Why They Happen to Good People*. Oxford: Oxford University Press.

Levy, Neil and Mandelbaum, Eric 2014: 'The Powers that Bind: Doxastic Voluntarism and Epistemic Obligation'. In Matheson, Jonathan and Vitz, Rico (eds.) *The Ethics of Belief*. Oxford: Oxford University Press, pp. 15–32.

Livingstone-Smith, David 2014: 'Self-Deception: A Teleofunctional Approach'. *Philosophia*. Vol. 42: pp. 181–99.

Machery, Edouard 2016: 'De-Freuding Implicit Attitudes'. In Brownstein, Michael and Saul, Jennifer (eds.) *Implicit Bias and Philosophy. Volume one. Metaphysics and Epistemology*. Oxford: Oxford University Press, pp. 104–29.

Madva, Alex 2016: 'Why Implicit Attitudes are (Probably) Not Beliefs'. *Synthese*. Vol. 193, pp. 2659–84.

Maher, Brendan 1974: 'Delusional Thinking and Perceptual Disorder'. *Journal of Individual Psychology*. Vol. 30, No. 1, 98–113.

Maher, Brendan 1988: 'Anomalous Experience and Delusional Thinking: The Logic of Explanations'. In Oltmanns, Thomas and Maher, Brendan (eds.) *Delusional Beliefs*. John Wiley and Sons, pp. 15–33.

Makinson, David C. 1965: 'The Paradox of the Preface'. *Analysis*. Vol. 25, no. 6, pp. 205–7.

Mandelbaum, Eric 2013: 'Against Alief'. *Philosophical Studies*. Vol. 165, pp. 197–211.

Mandelbaum, Eric 2016: 'Attitude, Inference, Association: On the Propositional Structure of Implicit Bias'. *Noûs*. Vol. 50, pp. 629–58.

Mandik, Peter 2007: 'Shit Happens'. *Episteme*. Vol. 4, no. 2, pp. 205–18.

Manktelow, Ken and Evans, Jonathan St B. T. 1979: 'Facilitation of Reasoning by Realism: Effect or Non-effect?' *British Journal of Psychology*. Vol. 70, no. 4, pp. 477–88.

McCormick, Miriam Schleifer 2015: *Believing Against the Evidence: Agency and the Ethics of Belief*. Abingdon: Routledge.

McIntyre, Alison 2006: 'What Is Wrong with Weakness of Will?' *The Journal of Philosophy*. Vol. 103, no. 6, pp. 284–311.

McKay, Ryan 2012: 'Delusional Inference'. *Mind & Language*. Vol. 27, no. 3, pp. 330–55.

McKay, Ryan 2015: 'Bayesian Accounts and Black Swans: Questioning the Erotetic Theory of Delusional Thinking'. *Cognitive Neuropsychiatry*. Vol. 20, no. 5, pp. 456–66.

McKay, Ryan and Mercier, Hugo 2023: 'Delusions as Epistemic Hypervigilance'. *Association for Psychological Science*. Vol. 32, no. 2, pp. 125–30.

McKenna, Peter 2017: *Delusions: Understanding the Un-understandable*. Cambridge:Cambridge University Press.

McKenna, Robin 2023: *Non-Ideal Epistemology*. Oxford: Oxford University Press.

McLaughlin, Brian 2009: 'Monothematic Delusions and Existential Feelings'. In Bayne, Tim and Fernández, Jordi (eds.) *Delusion and Self-Deception*. New York: Psychology Press, pp. 139–64.

Mele, Alfred 2001: *Self-Deception Unmasked*. Princeton: Princeton University Press.

Mele, Alfred 2009: 'Self-Deception and Delusions'. In Bayne, Tim and Fernandez, Jordi (Eds.) *Delusion and Self-Deception*. New York and London: Taylor and Francis, pp. 55–69.

Mishara, Aaron L. 2010: 'Klaus Conrad (1905–1961): Delusional Mood, Psychosis, and Beginning Schizophrenia'. *Schizophrenia Bulletin*. Vol. 36, no. 1, pp. 9–13.

Mitchell, Chris J., De Houwer, Jan, and Lovibond, Peter F. 2009: 'The Propositional Nature of Human Associative Learning'. *Behavioral and Brain Sciences*. Vol. 32, pp. 183–98.

Miyazono, Kengo, Bortolotti, Lisa, and Broome, Matthew 2014: 'Prediction-Error and Two-Factor Theories of Delusion Formation: Competitors or Allies?' In Galbraith, Neil (ed.) *Aberrant Beliefs and Reasoning*. Psychology Press, pp. 34–54.

Miyazono, Kengo and Salice, Alessandro 2021: 'Social Epistemological Conception of Delusion'. *Synthese*. Vol. 199, pp. 1831–51.

Murphy-Hollies, Kathleen and Caporuscio, Chiara 2023: 'What Is Left of Irrationality?' *Philosophical Psychology*. Vol. 36, no. 4, pp. 808–18.

Nanay, Bence 2021: 'Implict Bias as Mental Imagery'. *Journal of the American Philosophical Association*. Vol. 7, pp. 329–47.

Napolitano, M. Giulia 2021: 'Conspiracy Theories and Evidential Self-Insulation'. In Bernecker, Sven, Flowerree, Amy K. and Grundmann, Thomas (eds.) *The Epistemology of Fake News*. Oxford: Oxford University Press, pp. 82–105.

Nguyen, C. Thi 2020: 'Echo Chambers and Epistemic Bubbles'. *Episteme*. Vol. 17, no. 2, pp. 141–61.

Noordhof, Paul 2009: 'The Essential Instability of Self-Deception'. *Social Theory and Practice*. Vol. 35, no. 1, pp. 45–71.

Noordhof, Paul 2024a: 'Delusion and Doxasticism'. In Sullivan-Bissett, Ema (ed.) *The Routledge Handbook of Philosophy of Delusion*. Routledge. Oxon: Routledge, pp. 292–307.

Noordhof, Paul 2024b: 'Delusion and Doxasticism'. In Sullivan-Bissett, Ema (ed.) *The Routledge Handbook of Philosophy of Delusion*. Routledge. Oxon: Routledge, pp. 308–323.

Noordhof, Paul *manuscript*: 'Sub-Category Generalism About Conspiracy Theories'.

Noordhof, Paul and Sullivan-Bissett, Ema 2021: 'The Clinical Significance of Anomalous Experience in the Explanation of Delusion Formation'. *Synthese*. Vol. 199, pp. 10277–10309.

Noordhof, Paul and Sullivan-Bissett, Ema 2023: 'The Everyday Irrationality of Monothematic Delusion'. In Henne, Paul and Murray, Sam (eds.) *Advances in Experimental Philosophy of Action*. London: Bloomsbury, pp. 87–111.

Oswald, Frederick L., Mitchell, Gregory, Blanton, Hart, Jaccard, James, & Tetlock, Philip E. (2013). 'Predicting Ethnic and Racial Discrimination: A Meta-analysis of IAT Criterion studies'. *Journal of Personality and Social Psychology*. Vol. 105, no. 2, pp. 171–92.

Over, David E. and Evans, Jonathan St B. T. 2024: *Human Reasoning*. Cambridge: Cambridge University Press.

Payne, Keith B. and Gawronski, Bertram 2010: 'A History of Implicit Social Cognition: Where Is It Coming From? Where Is It Now? Where Is It Going?' In Gawronski, Bertram and Payne, Keith B. (eds.) *Handbook of Implicit Social Cognition: Measurement, Theory, and Applications*. New York: Guilford Press, pp. 1–15.

Pierre, Joseph M. 2020: 'Mistrust and Misinformation: A Two-Component, Socio-Epistemic Model of Belief in Conspiracy Theories'. *Journal of Social and Political Philosophy*. Vol. 8, no. 2, pp. 617–41.

Puddifoot, Katherine 2017: 'Dissolving the Epistemic/Ethical Dilemma over Implicit Bias'. *Philosophical Explorations*. Vol. 20, pp. 73–93.

Puddifoot, Katherine 2021: *How Stereotypes Deceive Us*. Oxford: Oxford University Press.

Reimer, Marga 2010: 'Only a Philosopher or a Madman: Impractical Delusions in Philosophy and Psychiatry'. *Philosophy, Psychiatry, & Psychology*. Vol. 17, no. 4, pp. 315–28.

Rey, Georges 1988: 'Toward a Computational Account of *Akrasia* and Self-Deception'. In Rorty, Amelie O. and McLaughlin, Brian P. (eds.) *Perspectives on Self-Deception*. Berkeley: University of California Press, pp. 264–96.

Rinard, Susanna 2017: 'No Exception for Belief'. *Philosophy and Phenomenological Research*. Vol. XCIV, no. 1, pp. 121–43.

Rorty, Amelie Oksenberg 1980: 'Where Does the Akratic Break Take Place?' *Australasian Journal of Philosophy*. Vol. 58, no. 94, pp. 333–46.

Ross, Robert M., Pennycook, Gordon, McKay, Ryan, Gervais, Will M., Langdon, Robyn, and Coltheart, Max 2016: 'Analytic Cognitive Style, Not Delusional Ideation, Predicts Data Gathering in a Large Beads Task Study'. *Cognitive Neuropsychiatry*. Vol. 21, no. 4, pp. 300–14.

Rysiew, Patrick 2008: 'Rationality Disputes – Psychology and Epistemology'. *Philosophy Compass*. Vol. 3, no. 6, pp. 1153–76.

Samuels, Richard, Stich, Stephen, and Faucher, Luc 2004: 'Reason and Rationality'. In Niiniluoto, I., Sintonen, M., and Woleński, J. (Eds.) *Handbook of Epistemology*, pp. 131–179.

Schroeder, Mark 2012: 'Stakes, Withholding, and Pragmatic Encroachment on Knowledge'. *Philosophical Studies*. Vol. 160, pp. 265–85.

Scott-Kakures, Dion 1996: 'Self-Deception and Internal Irrationality'. *Philosophy and Phenomenological Research*. Vol. 56, no. 1, pp. 31–56.

Sechrist, Gretchen and Stangor, Charles 2001: 'Perceived Consensus Influences Intergroup Behavior and Stereotype Accessibility'. *Journal of Personality and Social Psychology*. Vol. 80, no. 4, pp. 645–54.

Spaulding, Shannon 2015: 'Imagination, Desire, and Rationality'. *The Journal of Philosophy*. Vol. CXII, no. 9, pp. 457–76.

Stein, Edward 1997: *Without Good Reason: The Rationality Debate in Philosophy and Cognitive Science*. Oxford University Press.

Stone, Tony and Young, Andrew W. 1997: 'Delusions and Brain Injury: The Philosophy and Psychology of Belief', *Mind & Language*. Vol. 12, no. 3–4, pp. 327–64.

Stroud, Sarah and Tappolet, Christine 2003: 'Introduction'. In Stroud, Sarah and Tappolet, Christine (eds.) *Weakness of Will and Practical Irrationality*. Oxford University Press, pp. 1–16.

Sulik, Justin, Ross, Robert M., Balzan, Ryan, and McKay, Ryan 2023: 'Delusion-Like Beliefs and Data Quality: Are Classic Cognitive Biases Artifacts of Carelessness?' *Journal of Psychopathology and Clinical Science*. Vol. 132, no. 6, pp. 749–60.

Sullivan-Bissett, Ema 2015: 'Implicit Bias, Confabulation, and Epistemic Innocence'. *Consciousness and Cognition*. Vol. 33, pp. 548–60.

Sullivan-Bissett, Ema 2018: 'Monothematic Delusion: A Case of Innocence from Experience'. *Philosophical Psychology*. Vol. 31, no. 6, pp. 920–47.

Sullivan-Bissett, Ema 2019: 'Biased by Our Imaginings'. *Mind & Language*. Vol. 34, pp. 627–47.

Sullivan-Bissett, Ema 2020: 'Unimpaired Abduction to Alien Abduction: Lessons on Delusion Formation'. *Philosophical Psychology*. Vol. 33, no. 5, pp. 679–704.

Sullivan-Bissett, Ema 2022: 'Against a Second Factor'. *Asian Journal of Philosophy*. Vol. 1, article 33, pp. 1–10.

Sullivan-Bissett, Ema 2023: 'Implicit Bias and Processing'. In Thompson, Robert (ed.) *The Routledge Handbook of Implicit Cognition*. Routledge, pp. 115–25.

Sullivan-Bissett, Ema 2024: 'Introduction'. In Sullivan-Bissett, Ema (ed.) *The Routledge Handbook of the Philosophy of Delusion*. Routledge. Oxon: Routledge, pp. 1–29.

Sullivan-Bissett, Ema *forthcoming*: 'Evolutionary Pressures on Belief Capacities'. In Lombrozo, Tania and Van Leeuwen, Neil (eds.) *The Oxford Handbook of the Cognitive Science of Belief*.

Tetlock, Philip 2017: *Expert Political Judgment: How Good Is It? How Can We Know?* Princeton: Princeton University Press.

Tetlock, Philip, Kristel, Orie, Elson, Beth, Green, Melanie, and Lerner, Jennifer 2000: 'The Psychology of the Unthinkable: Taboo Trade-offs, Forbidden Base Rates, and Heretical Counterfactuals'. *Journal of Personality and Social Psychology*. Vol. 78, no. 5, pp. 853–70.

Thorstad, David 2024: 'Why Bounded Rationality (in Epistemology)?' *Philosophy and Phenomenological Research*. Vol. 102, no. 2, pp. 396–413.

Todd, Peter M. and Gigerenzer, Gerd 2012: *Ecological Rationality: Intelligence in the World*. New York: Oxford University Press.

Toribio, Josefa 2018: 'Implicit Bias: from Social Structure to Representational Format'. *Theoria*. Vol. 33, pp. 41–60.

Trope, Yaacov and Liberman, Akiva 1996: 'Social Hypothesis Testing: Cognitive and Motivational Mechanisms'. In Higgins, Edward T. and Kruglanski, Arie W. (eds.) *Social Psychology: Handbook of Basic Principles*. New York: Guilford Press, pp. 239–70.

Tversky, Amos and Kahneman, Daniel 1974: 'Judgment under Uncertainty: Heuristics and Biases'. *Science*. Vol. 185, no. 4157, pp. 1124–31.

Tversky, Amos and Kahneman, Daniel 1983: 'Extensional Versus Intuitive Reasoning: The Conjunction Fallacy in Probability Judgement'. *Psychological Review*. Vol. 90, pp. 293–315.

van der Wal, Reine C., Sutton, Robbie M., Lange, Jens, and Braga, Joao, P. N. 2018: 'Suspicious Binds: Conspiracy Thinking and Tenuous Perceptions of Causal Connections between Co-occurring and Spuriously Correlated Events'. *European Journal of Social Psychology*. Vol. 48, no. 7, pp. 970–89.

Van Leeuwen, Neil 2007: 'The Product of Self-Deception'. *Erkenntnis*. Vol. 67, pp. 419–37.

van Prooijen, Jan-Willem and Douglas, Karen M. 2018: 'Belief in Conspiracy Theories: Basic Principles of an Emerging Research Domain'. *European Journal of Social Psychology*. Vol. 48, no. 7, pp. 897–908.

van Prooijen, Jan-Willem, Wahring, Iris, Mausolf, Laura, Mulas, Nicole, and Shwan, Shayda 2023: 'Just Dead, Not Alive: Reconsidering Belief in Contradictory Conspiracy Theories'. *Psychological Science*. Vol. 34, no. 6, pp. 670–82.

Wason, Peter C. 1964: 'The Effect of Self-Contradiction on Fallacious Reasoning'. *Quarterly Journal of Experimental Psychology*. Vol. 16, pp. 30–4.

Wason, Peter C. 1966: 'Reasoning'. In Foss, Brian (ed.) *New Horizons in Psychology*. London: Penguin.

Wason, Peter C. and Shapiro, Diana 1971: 'Natural and Contrived Experience in a Reasoning Problem'. *Quarterly Journal of Experimental Psychology*. Vol. 23, pp. 63–71.

Williams, Daniel 2021: 'Socially Adaptive Belief'. *Mind & Language*. Vol. 36, pp. 333–54.

Williams, Daniel 2023: 'Bad Beliefs: Why they Happen to Highly Intelligent, Vigilant, Devious, Self-Deceiving, Coalitional Apes'. *Philosophical Psychology*. Vol. 36, no. 4, pp. 819–33.

Wood, Michael J., Douglas, Karen M., and Sutton, Robbie M. 2012: 'Dead and Alive: Beliefs in Contradictory Conspiracy Theories'. *Social Psychological and Personality Science*. Vol. 3, no. 6, pp. 767–73.

World Health Organisation 2023: 'World Health Statistics 2023'. www.who.int/data/stories/world-health-statistics-2023-a-visual-summary.

Yachanin, Stephen A. 1980: 'Differential Effects of Thematic Materials and Order of Rule Presentation on a Reasoning Task'. Unpublished Masters Thesis, Bowling Green State University.

Young, Andrew W., Robertson, Ian H., Hellawell, D. J., de Pauw, Karel W., and Pentland, Brian 1992: 'Cotard Delusion after Brain Injury'. *Psychological Medicine*, Vol. 22, pp. 799–804.

Young, Garry 2024: 'The Capgras Delusion: An Interactionist Approach Revisited'. In Sullivan-Bissett, Ema (ed.) *Belief, Imagination, and Delusion*. Oxford: Oxford University Press, pp. 151–182.

Acknowledgements

I acknowledge the Arts and Humanities Research Council (*Deluded by Experience*, grant no. AH/T013486/10) for funding my work. I am grateful to Keith Frankish for inviting me to write this Element, and for his very careful comments on the penultimate draft. Thank you also to two anonymous referees whose feedback on an earlier draft helped me improve the Element. Finally, thank you to Kathleen Murphy-Hollies, Michael Rush, Glen Sullivan-Bissett, Jessica Sutherland, and Sam Wilkinson for helpful comments.

Cambridge Elements

Philosophy of Mind

Keith Frankish
The University of Sheffield

Keith Frankish is a philosopher specializing in philosophy of mind, philosophy of psychology, and philosophy of cognitive science. He is the author of *Mind and Supermind* (Cambridge University Press, 2004) and *Consciousness* (2005), and has also edited or coedited several collections of essays, including *The Cambridge Handbook of Cognitive Science* (Cambridge University Press, 2012), *The Cambridge Handbook of Artificial Intelligence* (Cambridge University Press, 2014) (both with William Ramsey), and *Illusionism as a Theory of Consciousness* (2017).

About the Series

This series provides concise, authoritative introductions to contemporary work in philosophy of mind, written by leading researchers and including both established and emerging topics. It provides an entry point to the primary literature and will be the standard resource for researchers, students, and anyone wanting a firm grounding in this fascinating field.

Cambridge Elements

Philosophy of Mind

Elements in the Series

A full series listing is available at: www.cambridge.org/EPMI

www.ingramcontent.com/pod-product-compliance
Ingram Content Group UK Ltd.
Pitfield, Milton Keynes, MK11 3LW, UK
UKHW020125120225
454995UK00007B/25

9 781009 641906